COGNITIVE PSYCHOLOGY
RESEARCH DIRECTIONS IN
COGNITIVE SCIENCE
EUROPEAN PERSPECTIVES
Vol. 1

Cognitive Psychology
Research Directions in Cognitive Science
European Perspectives
Vol. 1

Edited by
Alan Baddeley
MRC Applied Psychology Unit,
15 Chaucer Road, Cambridge CB2 2EF,
England
and
Niels Ole Bernsen
Commission of the European Communities
Rue de la Loi 200
B-1049 Brussels,
Belgium

LAWRENCE ERLBAUM ASSOCIATES, PUBLISHERS
Hove and London (UK)   Hillsdale (USA)

Published on behalf of the Commission of the European Communities by:
Lawrence Erlbaum Associates Ltd., Publishers
27 Palmeira Mansions,
Church Road,
Hove,
East Sussex, BN3 2FA
U.K.

Publication No. EUR 11116 Vol. 1 of the
Commission of the European Communities,
Directorate-General Telecommunications, Information
Industries and Innovation,
Scientific and Technical Communication Service,
Luxembourg.

British Library Cataloguing in Publication Data

Reasearch directions in cognitive science: European perspectives.
Vol. 1, Cognitive psychology.
1. Cognitive psychology
I. Baddeley, Alan D. (Alan David), 1934-
153

ISBN 0-86377-111-4

Printed and bound by BPCC Wheatons, Exeter

Contents

General Introduction
A European Perspective
on Cognitive Science

Niels Ole Bernsen

ESPRIT Basic Research Actions
Commission of the European Communities
Rue de la Loi 200
B - 1049, Brussels, Belgium

The present volume on Cognitive Psychology is one in a series of five presenting the findings of a joint European study in cognitive science 1987-88. The study was organised and funded as a collaborative network by the research unit FAST (Forecast and Assessment in Science and Technology) of the Commission of the European Communities and comprised about 35 scientists from the core disciplines of cognitive science. The research disciplines represented in the network were: cognitive psychology, logic and linguistics, cognitive neuroscience, human–computer interaction, and artificial intelligence.

The aim of the network activity was to attempt a prospective mapping of research problems in cognitive science to be addressed over the next 5 – 10 years. Prospective judgment of course has to be based on firm knowledge of the state of the art but a presentation of the state-of-the-art of cognitive science as such was not our primary objective. This objective had already been addressed by a report presented to FAST in February 1986, *Cognitive Science in Europe* (ed. Michel Imbert et al.) and published by Springer-Verlag in October 1987.

As often happens in science nowadays, the dual aim of state-of-the-art presentation and prospective mapping realised through the FAST initiatives was linked to another, more practical aim, namely that of making sure that cognitive science finds its appropriate place in the European Community's long-term strategy for research and development in information technology. It is no doubt a pleasure to the contributors, and we hope to the European cognitive science community at large, that this has now happened to the extent that cognitive science has been included in the ESPRIT Basic Research Actions initiative, which forms the upstream, basic research complement to the European Communities ESPRIT programme in I.T. R. & D. In response to the first call for proposals for ESPRIT Basic Research Actions (1988), some $65-70 million are currently being committed to basic research in cognitive science and artificial intelligence, computer science, and microelectronics. Moreover, now that European cognitive science is becoming increasingly visible, partly through the FAST and ESPRIT initiatives, it seems reasonable to expect an increase in cognitive science funding at the national level.

As part of the more practical aim of funding procurement, the network agenda also included surveying and commenting upon the current institutional state and the state of collaboration in European cognitive science. Results and, we hope, some timely recommendations form part of a separate report of the network activity (Bernsen & the FAST Network, 1988).

The overall view of cognitive science taken in the papers published in the present volumes is fairly comprehensive though not exhaustive. Choice of topics for presentation and discussion has been made with a view to potential long-term relevance to information technology. Authors have been encouraged to take a personal view of their respective fields rather than a more comprehensive, and perhaps less exciting, encyclopaedic view. Each contribution has been written in order to make it comprehensible to cognitive scientists from other disciplines.

Since the general characteristics of current cognitive science are not, as such, addressed in the individual introductions or papers, a brief sketch may be in place here.

Sometimes a new theory can provide a unifying perspective to a number of hitherto disparate scientific endeavours and thus motivate a potentially drastic regrouping among the sciences. This is the case in cognitive science, where a new theory of the most general type which I shall call a *research programme* currently has this effect. The new research programme offering a unifying perspective to large parts of the sciences of logic, linguistics, psychology and neuroscience came from computer science and artificial intelligence and had been gaining ground steadily since the 1950s. It consists of the general idea that intelligent agents should be looked upon as information processing systems, that is, as systems receiving, manipulating, storing, retrieving, transmitting and executing information. Some of the general questions to ask concerning intelligent agents according to this research programme are: what information do such systems have? how is it represented? how is the information processed? and how are the processes implemented? The theoretical language of cognitive science is that of computation and information processing.

The objectives of cognitive science are to define, build and test information processing models of the various sub-systems (and of *their* sub-systems) making up an intelligent agency, whether human (biological, natural) or artificial, and eventually to make them fit together into general cognitive theories and systems. The knowledge obtained can then be applied in various ways. Examples of cognitive sub-systems are vision, speech, natural language, sensory–motor control, memory, learning and reasoning. Each of these sub-systems is highly complex and may be further broken down into a number of functional components. Today's limited-capacity autonomous robots and knowledge based systems having a (written or spoken) natural language interface are examples of technologically implemented steps towards more general systems.

In somewhat more detail, the research programme of cognitive science may be characterised as follows:

1. Intelligence or cognition is physically implemented. However, a central level of analysis is the description of cognitive systems as systems for the manipulation of representations. Representations may consist of discrete symbols or may be of other types such as distributed representations.

2. Widely different types of physical implementation are capable, in principle, of manipulating the same representations in the same ways: chips made of silicon or galliumarsenide, optical devices, mechanical, or hydraulic devices, organic–biological systems.

3. Artificial, i.e. non-biological intelligence and hyperintelligence is therefore possible, at least in principle. Cognitive science is an investigation of both biological and artificial intelligence.

4. The level of description at which cognitive systems are described as manipulating representations cannot be reduced to:

(a) the physical implementation of the system ;
(b) the behaviour of the system ;
(c) the conscious experiences of the system, if any.

5. Cognitive science is mechanistic. Intelligence or cognition, including semantics or meaning, and consciousness, is regarded as being produced by, in a wide sense, mechanical operations.

6. Acceptance of some version of functionalism. Functionalism states that cognition is constituted by the information processing functions which are physically implemented in the system.

7. Historically as well as in scientific substance and methodology, cognitive science is closely related to the computer and its information processing potential as studied by computer science and artificial intelligence. The paradigms of cognitive science still derive from contemporary computer systems, whether serial or parallel, classical or connectionist. Use of computer simulations is essential to cognitive science except for the few areas, like problems involving social or organisational aspects, where specific computer modelling is not yet feasible.

8. Cognitive science is multidisciplinary. Methodologically, cognitive science aims at increased collaboration and cross-fertilisation between disciplines, the central assumption being that this is the most promising way of accelerating the achievement of the research programme, and hence also of realising the application potential of cognitive science. If anything has become apparent over the last 20 years, it is that

cognition or intelligence are extremely complex phenomena whose investigation requires the full exploitation of a wide range of methodological tools. The basic idea behind the interdisciplinarity of cognitive science, then, is that each discipline employs its own *particular* methods in order to add *constraints* to the construction of *common* models and theories of the cognitive functions and their interrelationships. These models and theories are expressed in the common language of cognitive science, that is, in the language of the research programme and of one or other of the paradigms (discussed later). In addition, the basic idea behind interdisciplinarity assumes that each discipline could significantly contribute to the development of models and theories. So each discipline should, in order to belong to cognitive science, be concerned with both knowledge and processing (or competence and performance) in cognition, abstract programme and implementation, peripheral and central processes, sub-system integration, and the understanding of intelligent performance in complex, real-life tasks.

Present-day cognitive science is an interdisciplinary endeavour rather than a new science in its own right, and speaking about core disciplines suggests that insights from other sciences like mathematics, physics, biology, computer science, anthropology, and the philosophy of science, mind and language actually do contribute to the advance of cognitive science. Furthermore, numerous sub-disciplines exist linking the core disciplines together, such as computational linguistics, computational logic, psycholinguistics, neuropsychology, and so on.

9. Cognitive science is closely related to application, in particular, though not exclusively, to the application of information technology. Applications of cognitive science are of at least three types.

(a) Specifying information processing models of the various sub-systems making up intelligent agency is essential to the building of increasingly intelligent artifacts such as the coming generations of vision systems, speech systems, natural language interfaces, robots, and knowledge-based systems. Interactions between the various disciplines of cognitive science have in the past produced such important AI knowledge representation and reasoning techniques as semantic networks, production systems, and logic programming, as well as significant results in areas like vision, speech and natural language processing. Future interaction will have to face still other areas of research where humans continue to perform far better than current artificial systems, as in causal reasoning, reasoning about time, plans and intentions, learning, or fluent, skill-based behaviour.

(b) It has become clear that the actual design of information processing systems should go hand in hand with research on their interactions with human agents in real-life task situations. Through the computerisation of work in all sectors of society, information technology has become an important tool at the interface between humans and their work. Successful system design, whether of large control systems, computer networks, manufacturing systems, office systems, tutoring systems, speech and language systems, or expert systems, not only depends on the training of users but also on the systems' inherent adaptability to users. If a system's design is not successful, users are not likely to want to use it, and if they do use it, serious accidents may occur, as in nuclear power plants or large chemical installations. In this situation, cognitive science research is strongly needed in the interaction between I.T. tools, task domain and work context, the cognitive resources of users, and the new patterns of social interaction arising from the use of computers. Thus, the rapidly evolving field of human–computer interaction research could be included among the core disciplines making up cognitive science as being sufficiently distinct from, and somewhat orthogonal to, the others to merit a disciplinary label of its own.

(c) Although these two points describing the application potential of cognitive science for information technology have been central to the present network activity, it should be noted that they do not exhaust the application potential of cognitive science. The human information processing system can be damaged or inoperative in various ways and from various causes, with neurological and psychological disorders or loss of certain mental abilities as a result. Studying the system and its behaviour in information processing terms promises better ways for diagnosing, repairing, and retraining the system as well as better ways of supplying the system with efficient prostheses.

The aforementioned points 1–9 are by no means uncontroversial among cognitive scientists. And needless to say, interdisciplinary collaboration among traditionally separate disciplines is not uncontroversial either. What is interesting, however, is that points 1–9 currently do seem to represent international convergence towards a common conception of cognitive science.

A research programme is in itself nothing very important. What matters are the research paradigm(s) demonstrating the practical viability of the programme. A research paradigm consists of one or more successful, specific applications of the research programme to particular problems falling within its scope. These applications, *in casu* models of specific cognitive functions, are seen by the scientific community as evidence that the principles on which they are based might be generalised to account for a much larger class of cognitive phenomena, and possibly to all of cognition. The central scientific task, then, is to implement and test this assumption. Cognitive science currently appears to have to consider two different research paradigms. The relationship between them is not clear at this point and is subject to strong, ongoing debate (e.g. Fodor & Pylyshyn, 1988; Smolensky, 1988).

According to the *Classical AI* paradigm, an intelligent system's input and output consist of physical signals and movements, whereas a large central part of the information processing linking input and output consists of automatic computation over language-like, discrete, and combinatorial symbolic codes, as in conventional serial or more recent parallel computers (Fodor, 1976; Newell, 1980; Pylyshyn, 1984). According to the *Neural Network Computation* paradigm or the *Connectionist* paradigm, which has been strongly revived in the 1980s, computation over discrete combinatorial symbols exists to a lesser extent, or does not exist at all, in intelligent biological systems. Instead, the complex cognitive abilities of higher organisms are based on the information processing abilities arising from the collective behaviour of large populations of highly interconnected and very simple processing elements such as nerve cells or simple artificial processing elements. Consequently, it is maintained, cognitive scientists should develop and implement their theories of intelligent information processing in ways that resemble much more closely the way in which the brain actually operates (McClelland & Rumelhart, 1986).

Today, both paradigms can claim a number of successes in terms of concrete models jointly covering most areas of cognitive science.

This ongoing debate over research paradigms is a very real one because, at the present time at least, the two paradigms clearly do generate different systems providing different functional primitives (i.e. different elementary information processing capabilities) and possibly different behaviours.

Thus, the virtues of connectionist systems include their ability to rapidly acquire and apply large amounts of knowledge in noisy situations not governed by rigid laws but by context–sensitive regularities having many exceptions. And the paradigms generate importantly different directions for research and different technologies, and tend to attract different core disciplines of cognitive science. Thus, many researchers in classical AI tend to be sceptical about the potential of artificial neural network systems, despite the success of similar systems in nature; others do not doubt the importance for AI of "massive parallelism", but argue that connectionist systems do not really represent an alternative research paradigm, only a specific way of physically implementing classical cognitive architectures. Logicians and most linguists tend to disregard connectionist systems, whereas many cognitive psychologists and virtually all cognitive neuroscientists, who never really adopted the classical AI paradigm anyway, tend to embrace the neural network computation paradigm as the first firm basis for realistic models and general theories of cognition. The formal language of the classical AI paradigm is that of symbolic logic and algebra, whereas the formal language of the connectionist paradigm is that of dynamic systems theory belonging to mathematical physics. Also, researchers studying the peripherals of cognitive systems like speech, low-level vision, or movement, all of which involve considerable signal processing, appear to be more strongly attracted by neural network computation than those studying central processes. Not least, this latter point has led many cognitive scientists to believe that the two paradigms really are basically different cognitive architectures, but that they are compatible in the sense of being apt to model different types of cognitive function or different parts of cognitive functions, such as voluntary, introspectively accessible, attentive, and controlled processes versus skilled, automatic, pre-attentive, probably massively parallel processes. Research in the next 5–10 years will no doubt result in important attempts to integrate these two approaches or paradigms of cognitive science.

Two interrelated themes dominate the network findings and cut across the distinction between scientific substance and methodology. These themes can be viewed as constituting some central tendencies of current research covering all the core disciplines of cognitive science. Since the themes or trends are based on prospective analyses of most areas of cognitive science, from research on vision and speech to research on natural language, logic, and reasoning, they appear to form a stable pattern. These trends should be encouraged by an appropriate research policy.

The themes are *integration* in theory, computer models, and actual working implementations, and *real-world validity* of theories, models and applications.

The theme of integration covers the following aspects:

Integration of different cognitive functions;
Integration of cognitive sub-functions into cognitive functions;
Integration of models into more general theories;
Integration of partial models into full models;
Integration and convergence of approaches, methods, and results from different disciplines;
A more theory-driven approach in traditionally experimental disciplines like cognitive psychology and neuroscience.

Integration clearly means a trend towards the construction and testing of general theories and towards increased interdisciplinarity. Moreover, as mentioned earlier, the possibility of integrating the two current research paradigms of cognitive science is currently the subject of lively debates.

The real-world theme covers the trend towards explaining, simulating and actually building larger-scale, more general-purpose, real-time, closer-to-real-life systems of speech and grammar, natural language and communication, vision, perception and movement or action, and problem-solving. This trend also receives strong support from human–computer interaction research, which from the outset has to face human information processing in complex, real-life situations. Real-world research in cognitive science contrasts with, e.g., research in cognitive psychology on the performance of abstract and ecologically meaningless tasks in the laboratory or AI research on system performance in "micro-worlds". The real-world trend marks an important step beyond these classical approaches in cognitive science and implies the disappearance from the field of the sharp, traditional distinction between basic and applied research.

The two themes of integration and real-world validity are closely related because, in a large number of cases, explanation and synthesis of performance in complex, real-life situations require an integration of different cognitive functions and systems, and of different approaches. The themes are also closely related to the technological applicability of models, systems, and theories because integration and real-world validity is what is needed, both in order to extend the range of applicability of systems and in order to adapt them to users. In many cases, computer simulations may function both as theoretical test-beds and as software prototypes of potential machines for technological applications.

Numerous examples of the above trends can be gathered from the network papers. I shall leave it to the reader to find these examples and to judge whether they are sufficient to justify the conclusions stated above. If they are, then it can confidently be stated that contemporary cognitive science in Europe demonstrates the viability of the research programme, the productivity of the research paradigms, the convergence of disciplines towards common models, theories and problems to the extent allowed by the existence of two different paradigms, and the potential applicability of results. Not everything is idyllic, however; nor could or should this be so within an emerging science. Most of the basic questions still remain unanswered, with the prospect that cognitive science may look very different in 10 years time.

I would like to warmly thank all network participants for their friendly collaboration during the past two years. We all learned, I think, that even today, large-scale, multidisciplinary European collaboration in science is not a matter of course, but something that requires a substantial effort. I am especially grateful to the leaders of the four "network institutions" and the Special Editors of the first four volumes in the series: Alan Baddeley (Cambridge APU), Michel Imbert (University Paris VI), Jens Rasmussen (Riso National Laboratory), and Helmut Schnelle (Bochum University). Without their judgment, vigilance, patience and collaborative spirit the network would never have been set up, let alone have produced anything. Derek Sleeman (Aberdeen), Special Editor of Volume V, entered the collaboration at a later stage and has demonstrated impressive efficiency in catching up with the work that had already been done.

We are all deeply indebted to Dr Riccardo Petrella, Head of FAST, whose sensitivity to emerging trends in science and technology first brought cognitive science to the attention of EC scientific programmes and whose dynamism, non-hesitant support, and constant good-will have made the network possible. I must personally thank Dr Petrella and the Danish Science and Engineering Research Council for making my one-year stay at FAST possible, and the EC's ESPRIT programme for allowing me time to complete the work while assisting in setting up the ESPRIT Basic Research Actions.

REFERENCES

Bernsen, N.O. & the FAST Cognitive Science Network (1988). *Cognitive science: A European perspective*. (Report to the FAST Programme.) FAST, EC Commission, Brussels.

Fodor, J.A. & Pylyshyn, Z.W.(1988). Connectionism and cognitive architecture. *Cognition, 28*, (1–2), 3–71.

Fodor, J.A.(1976). *The Language of Thought*. Sussex: The Harvester Press.

Imbert, M., Bertelson, P., Kempson, R., Osherson, D., Schnelle, H., Streitz, N.A., Thomassen, A., & Viviani, P. (Eds.)(1987). *Cognitive Science in Europe*. Springer-Verlag.

McClelland, J.L., Rumelhart, D.E. & the PDP Research Group (Eds.) (1986). *Parallel Distributed Processing* Vols. 1–2, Cambridge MA: Bradford Books, MIT Press.

Newell, A.(1980). Physical Symbol Systems, *Cognitive Science, 4*, 135–183.

Pylyshyn, Z.W.(1984). *Computation and Cognition. Toward a Foundation for Cognitive Science*. Bradford Books, Cambridge MA, MIT Press.

Smolensky, P.(1988). On the proper treatment of connectionism. *Behavioral and Brain Sciences, 11* (1), 1–74.

CHAPTER 1

Cognitive Psychology and Cognitive Science

Alan Baddeley

*MRC Applied Psychology Unit, 15 Chaucer Road,
Cambridge CB2 2EF,
England*

INTRODUCTION

The purpose of this initial chapter is to give a brief introduction to what follows. It tries to explain how the pieces that constitute the rest of the book came to be written, why the particular topics and particular authors were selected, and why I should be the person editing a book on cognitive science. This will be followed by a brief and again rather personal view of the relationship between cognitive psychology and cognitive science. This chapter does not therefore represent an introduction to either cognitive psychology or cognitive science.

As Bernsen has already explained, these papers were the result of an initiative by the section of the European Community concerned with Forecasting and Assessment in Science and Technology (FAST). It was proposed that a small working party be given the task of reviewing research on cognitive science, with the aim of encouraging the European Community to fund a major research programme in this area. A number of individuals and institutions were asked if they would be responsible for co-ordinating the survey in their own particular area. I was asked if the Applied Psychology Unit (APU) and myself would be prepared to co-ordinate the review of cognitive psychology.

My initial inclination was to refuse. The time-scale requested was set by the need to feed the information into the political system within a very few months, and seemed ridiculously short. The task seemed daunting, and one that was almost certain to offend more people than it pleased. But, on the other hand, I do have a strong commitment to European collaboration in science and saw this as an important opportunity.

At a scientific level I also had doubts. I tended not to think of myself as a cognitive

1

scientist; I regarded the term *cognitive science* as a synonym for artificial intelligence, an area in which I can certainly claim no expertise. The request came, however, while I was attending a U.S. Office of Naval Research contractors meeting, as a guest. I was impressed and excited by a number of the papers linking AI and cognitive psychology, in particular those using a connectionist approach to modelling cognitive data using parallel distributed processing systems. What impressed me was the extent to which the models suggested empirical experiments, together with possible ways of reconceptualising old theoretical problems. The models were based on empirical data and spoke very directly to some of the classical problems of cognitive psychology. They reinforced my conviction that cognitive psychology, with its emphasis on empirical evidence collected under well controlled conditions, was an important complement to artificial intelligence, and that both were contributors to a broader field, a field that it seems appropriate to refer to as cognitive science.

Computational methods have played, and will continue to play, a central role in cognitive science, but they need to be tested and evaluated by rules of empirical evidence, the domain of cognitive psychology. The computer has already had a major impact on the development of theory in cognitive psychology, and computer simulation is in future likely to play an even greater role, but to define any area, including cognitive science in terms of a single piece of equipment or a single method, however powerful, is ultimately likely to lead to sterility.

Therefore, as a cognitive psychologist I believe that I am part of the broader area known as cognitive science. I also believe that the empirical approach of cognitive psychology is complementary to the exciting new developments in computation. Bearing that in mind, I decided that it was important that mainstream cognitive psychology should be involved in the FAST initiative. I talked to my colleagues at the APU, and ascertained that they supported the idea, and having failed to find anyone else who would take on the job of co-ordination, I decided to accept the invitation.

The initial constraints were to review the area of cognitive psychology, with particular emphasis on those aspects that might persuade the European Community that it would be wise, both scientifically and commercially, to invest in research in cognitive science. In short, it seemed appropriate to attempt to emphasize links with the increasingly important information technology industry. In selecting and instructing reviewers, I encouraged the enthusiastic pursuit of a particular approach, rather than a judicious and balanced overview, since at this point, the aim was to enthuse some unspecified Eurocrat, Eurotechnician or Euroscientist, rather than to give an overview for fellow scholars. One final and overriding constraint was that of time. The contributors had to be people who I could persuade to accept a demanding and somewhat thankless task, to be completed within unrealistic time constraints. As the number of British, and indeed APU, authors in this volume indicates, my powers of persuasion tended to decrease with distance, leading inevitably to a review that has a much less broad European authorship than I would have chosen, given other circumstances.

After discussion with other participants in the FAST initiative, and with my colleagues at APU, we decided to opt for reviews of a number of areas, each chosen as having a potentially useful link between cognitive psychology, cognitive science and information technology on the one hand, and having sufficient research strength in Europe to justify an injection of new funding, on the other.

The areas we chose were as follows. Vision was one obvious choice, with a strong European tradition, considerable existing links between cognitive psychology, psychophysics and artificial intelligence, together with an obvious area of application in computer vision and robotics. Brian Rogers from Oxford and Roger Watt from my own Unit agreed to cover this area. We hesitated about whether or not it would be necessary to cover acoustics, because it was possible that this area would be adequately covered by the FAST group concerned with logic and linguistics. We subsequently decided that there remained a gap in this area and asked Roy Patterson and Anne Cutler from the APU to try to cover the interface area between psychoacoustics, traditionally concerned with signal processing, and the more linguistically based research on speech perception, an area of considerable potential applicability in connection with automatic speech recognition.

Learning and memory is a central area of cognitive psychology, and one that has become particularly exciting with the recent development of parallel distributed processing models. We invited Bill Phillips from Stirling to write about this, knowing that he was enthusiastically working in this area as a cognitive psychologist, collaborating with both computer scientists and neurophysiologists. It was felt that in following his brief, Bill had produced something that was a powerful argument for a particular approach, but that it should be put in a slightly broader context. I myself agreed to do this, with a further section on machine learning, a topic that neither of us felt able to cover, provided by my colleague Richard Young. Psycholinguistics provided another area of obvious importance within both cognitive psychology and potentially within information technology. I was pleased to be able to persuade Leo Noordman to cover this area, bearing in mind the links with other chapters in the Logic and Linguistics section of the review.

Of the many other areas of cognitive psychology, we clearly needed something on thinking, reasoning and decision taking, all topics that are both central to cognitive psychology, and also of potential applicability in the information technology area, notably in the rapidly developing field of expert systems. We initially asked John Fox of the Imperial Cancer Research Fund, London, to cover this rather broad area from the twin perspectives of cognitive psychology and artificial intelligence. Not unreasonably, he found this an impossible task within the constraints set, and we therefore split the area, asking John Fox to concentrate on the relationship between AI and cognitive psychology, and Jonathan Evans of Plymouth to undertake the task of reviewing work on thinking, reasoning and decision making, requiring him to operate under what was by now an even shorter time-scale, a challenge he was fortunately prepared to accept.

By this point we had reached the number of contributors that could be permitted to cover cognitive psychology. Two areas we would otherwise have certainly had to cover

CP—B

were motor skills and neuropsychology, but Michel Imbert agreed that both these areas would be covered in his section of the initiative by authors who would be acceptable to both the neuroscience and cognitive psychology groups, and they will duly be covered in the Neurosciences volume of this series. Similarly, work on various aspects of applied cognitive psychology will be covered in the volume on Human–Computer interaction, while the Logic and Linguistics volume has a number of chapters of direct relevance to psycholinguistics and language processing.

Having hurriedly set up this series of reviews, we were subsequently informed that the case for funding cognitive science that we had hoped to make had already been conceded by the European Community, who decided to fund basic research in the area of cognitive science under the planned ESPRIT Basic Research Actions, which was to form the basic research complement to the more applied ESPRIT programme of pre-competetive research initiative in the area of information technology. Meanwhile, we were still tasked to report to FAST, which in due course we did.

Having done so, the question arose as to what should happen to our reviews. Should they simply be lodged with the EEC or should they be given wider circulation? On balance, we felt that perhaps they would be of interest to colleagues in cognitive psychology and related disciplines. It should be emphasized, however, that the chapters that follow are not offered as a prescription for what the EEC should or would fund; we have absolutely no role in the funding process. Nor are they intended as balanced, thorough and scholarly overviews of the major areas of cognitive psychology, but rather as personal statements by a number of active cognitive psychologists about their field, and how they themselves see their subject and its possible contribution to the development of cognitive science.

The remainder of this chapter offers a brief, limited and personal overview of an important and complex topic, that of the relationship between cognitive science and cognitive psychology.

COGNITIVE ENGINEERING AND COGNITIVE SCIENCE

I use the term cognitive science to imply the study of principles underlying cognition, together with its instantiation in the operation of brains, minds and machines. Its success is judged by the extent to which it can give a satisfactory account of the way in which brains and minds actually work. Cognitive engineering, on the other hand, is assumed to be concerned with the development of machines that will perform the type of cognitive task that was previously regarded as the prerogative of people and animals. As a branch of engineering, its success is judged by the capacities of such devices to perform the tasks in question, regardless of whether the tasks are performed in the same way by the machine as by biological systems, such as the human brain. Hence, as a piece of cognitive engineering, current chess playing computer programs are relatively successful since they are capable of beating all but the most expert players. As examples of cognitive science, however, they are much less so, because they operate in ways that differ very markedly from that of a human chess player (Holding, 1985).

The information technology industry is, of course, primarily concerned with cognitive engineering. Why, then, should it be interested in cognitive science? Let me begin by rejecting one argument; I do not wish to argue that the best way of programming a computer to perform a cognitive task is to study the way in which the brain solves that task and simulate it. As proponents of artificial intelligence frequently point out, the development of successful aeroplanes was not based on the detailed analysis of flight in birds. So why is cognitive science of interest to cognitive engineers?

First, the fact that the problem can be solved by the brain demonstrates that it is soluble, and the way in which the human being solves it may certainly offer useful hypotheses. In some cases, these may be directly modified to solve a practical problem, as for example in the case of expert systems based on the production system architecture devised by Newell and Simon as part of their general problem solving model.

Secondly, developments in basic research may sometimes have a quite unexpected but potentially very important subsequent application. Such serendipitous findings may have a relatively low probability of successful application, but when applicability does occur, it can be of enormous practical significance, often precisely because it involves findings that would not have emerged using existing applied techniques. I suspect that some of the connectionist learning algorithms currently under development may prove to fall into this category. To take a specific example, the parallel distributed processing models developed in the experimental psychology laboratory to simulate tasks such as reading, or to perform simple learning algorithms already seem to have great promise as expert systems, capable, for instance, of learning sensory discriminations that humans find difficult. The development of a connectionist system that can learn to detect and discriminate sonar signals is one example of this (Gorman and Sejnowski, in press), and it seems likely that in due course similar models will be devised to perform a wide range of difficult perceptual tasks such as reading X-rays or signature verification.

A third important aspect of cognitive science is to offer challenging and flexible training for future cognitive engineers. As such it should reduce the danger that the field will become stuck in lines of development that guarantee safe solutions to tractable problems, but retard long-term progress.

Finally, the products of information technology typically have to be used by people, as the many major problems in the area of human–computer interaction testify. Failure to map the machine on to the user is a massive source of system failure, and system usability is likely to be a major determinant of the marketability of information technology systems in the future. At present, designers probably rely largely on their own intuitions. That branch of cognitive science known sometimes as cognitive ergonomics promises a rather more satisfactory basis for system design.

THE STRUCTURE OF COGNITIVE SCIENCE

The term cognitive science refers to the study of the general principles whereby systems perform such tasks as perceiving, learning, remembering, deciding, using language and solving problems. As such, it is an area in which a number of other disciplines overlap, including the neurosciences, logic, linguistics, computer science and psychology. Figure 1 shows one way of conceptualising this relationship, proposed by Smolensky (1987) in a paper concerned primarily with discussing the relationship between two styles of modelling within artificial intelligence, one based on serial symbol processing models and the other based on connectionist or parallel distributed processing architectures.

Smolensky suggests that cognitive science is concerned with the study of the way in which featuresof mental life such as plans, goals, strategies, percepts and memories are related to the underlying neural architecture. He suggests that the links occur at two levels. One of these involves the study of the architecture of cognition at a precise and detailed level that he refers to as "subsymbolic". He suggests that the connectionist approach operates at this level. The other which he terms the "symbolic" level provides a more macro and more approximate level of analysis. This he associates with symbol processing approaches to artificial intelligence.

A related point is made by Pylyshyn (1984), who distinguishes between components of cognitive performance that are "cognitively penetrable", that is those that are open to introspection and can be influenced by the introspective subject, and those that are "impenetrable". The operation of impenetrable components is not open

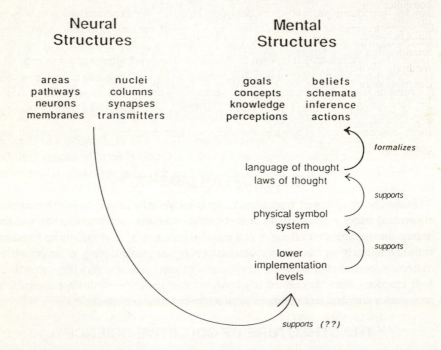

FIG. 1.1   Neural and mental structures in the symbolic paradigm.

to introspection and they are not subject to conscious modification. The direction of visual attention, or the selection and operation of a learning strategy would be examples of "penetrable" processes, whereas the operation of stereopsis, or the process whereby an item is retrieved from long-term memory, would probably fall into the "impenetrable" category. It seems possible at least that the penetrable level of analysis is broadly characteristic of the symbol processing level, whereas connectionist models are concerned with the architecture of cognition at the impenetrable level (Johnson-Laird, 1988). It seems unlikely that there would be general agreement on this point, but the issue is one that is likely to be an important one in cognitive science over the next few years.

COGNITIVE PSYCHOLOGY AND COGNITIVE SCIENCE

What differentiates the contribution to cognitive science made by psychology as opposed to that of artificial intelligence, logic, linguistics or neuroscience? It differs from neuroscience in not being primarily concerned with the neural structures, but rather with their function. The relationship between neural structure and cognitive function is relevant to cognitive psychology, and comprises the currently very active field known as cognitive neuropsychology. Cognitive psychology differs from A.I. and computer science, on the other hand, in having a stronger concern for the empirical investigation of cognitive phenomena, although at a theoretical level there are strong links between cognitive psychology and A.I. In the case of linguistics, there are again relationships with cognitive psychology, but also basic differences in both aims and methods. Whereas linguistics is primarily concerned with providing a formal description of language, often appealing to linguistic intuition in order to decide between alternative possibilities, psycholinguistics, as a branch of cognitive psychology, is less concerned with a description of language as a formal structure, and more concerned with empirical questions of how humans actually generate and comprehend language.

THE EUROPEAN DIMENSION

The areas to be reviewed were chosen partly for their combination of practical and theoretical relevance, and partly because sufficient European strength and expertise exists in these areas for effective major programmes to be mounted. It is, however, only realistic to accept that the distribution of expertise in cognitive psychology within Europe is somewhat patchy.

In the early years of experimental psychology, the contribution of German research was paramount, and that of France also relatively strong. In the last 20 or 30 years, however, the psychology of much of Europe, including Germany and France, has been most strongly influenced by non-experimental approaches, with clinical psychology often being the dominant theme. During this period, the field was dominated, in terms of sheer output at least, by North American psychology, although that in turn has been influenced by the information processing tradition which has had some of its strongest roots in Europe, and in particular in Britain.

There are encouraging signs that cognitive psychology within Europe is beginning to grow in strength and confidence. A European Society for Cognitive Psychology has just been founded and recently held its third general conference and its first Summer School. Cognitive psychology is beginning to thrive in countries such as Spain and Portugal which, until the recent changes in the regimes of these countries, appeared to be very weak in psychology, while in Italy, degrees in psychology as a separate subject have begun to appear, promising a possible end to the split there between psychology as a branch of medicine and psychology as a branch of education. It is becoming increasingly clear that excellent European groups exist, often carrying out lively innovative work within traditions that appeared to have been lost. The sheer volume of North American work is finally leading to English being accepted as a common language, with the result that language barriers should be less of a handicap than they have been in the past.

A major problem in many European countries however remains that of isolation, with too few first-rate workers spread too thinly. If cognitive psychology in Europe is to achieve anything like its potential, it is essential to increase collaboration, and to move from the present situation, where many Europeans see their main links with colleagues in North America, to a situation in which more and stronger European collaborative links are fostered.

All the research areas I have discussed would benefit from collaboration between at least two, and often several countries. It is important to set up a network structure that will allow links and visits to be set up without being tied to too much bureaucracy. I believe that in the long term, it will be contacts at the level of collaboration between individual scientists in different disciplines and different countries that will determine the future of cognitive science in Europe, and trust that the FAST initiative that led to these reports will be the beginning of a period of increasing collaboration across disciplines and across countries as part of the development of a strong and lively European cognitive science community.

REFERENCES

Gorman, R.P. and Sejnowski, T.J. (in press). Learned classification of sonar targets using a massively-parallel network. IEEE Transactions in Acoustics and Speech Signal Processing.

Holding, D.H. (1985). The Psychology of Chess Skill. Hillsdale, N.J.: Lawrence Erlbaum Associates Inc.

Johnson-Laird, P.N. (1988). The Computer and the Mind. An Introduction to cognitive science. London: Fontana.

Pylyshyn, Z. (1984). Computation and Cognition. Toward a Foundation for cognitive science. Cambridge, Mass.: MIT Press.

Smolensky, P. (1987). Connectionist AI, symbolic AI, and the brain. Artificial Intelligence Review, 1, 95-109.

CHAPTER 2

Human Vision and Cognitive Science

R.J. Watt

MRC Applied Psychology Unit, 15 Chaucer Road, Cambridge CB2 2EF, England

B.J. Rogers

Department of Experimental Psychology, South Parks Road, Oxford OX1 3UD, England

The study of vision is a paradigmatic cognitive science. The eyes generate multi-dimensional signals, which are then examined for information relevant to the many tasks collectively known as perception. This is only possible because the properties of matter in the world are constrained; the processes of visual perception depend upon those constraints. Tasks, constraints, information, signals and the relationships between them are characteristic of all cognitive sciences.

Progress towards understanding vision is currently being made in the distinct fields of computer science, robotics, psychophysics, psychology and physiology. In this paper we argue that the logico-formal linking hypotheses between these disciplines need to be explored in order to allow collaboration. Key conceptual issues that remain unsolved are identified and means by which they might be explored are considered. It is argued that the concepts involved are, at an abstract level, germane to the whole enterprise of cognitive science.

9

INTRODUCTION: WHAT IS VISION?

We perceive the physical environment that we inhabit, the relationships between the things in that environment, and the relationships between those things and ourselves. We do so in order that we may interact appropriately with the environment. This is the purpose of perception.

Perception is inherently limited because the sensory organs, especially those of vision, touch and hearing, deliver signals which simply reflect the spatial and temporal patterns of certain types of energy on certain sensory surfaces. These signals, could in principle, have arisen in an infinite number of ways. However, the patterns preserve some clues to the spatial structure of the scene and with the aid of a priori knowledge (procedural and also declarative) of how our world is constrained we are able to interact coherently and consistently with the environment.

Suppose that you move to catch a ball. As the ball flies through the air towards you, there are changes in the corresponding parts of the retinal image. Since the image is just a distribution of light energy in space and time, it is misleading to state that the image of the ball increases in size. All that is actually explicit in the image is the temporal patterns of light intensity at different spatial positions. If we can justifiably assume that matter is generally continuous, cohesive, opaque and stable, then it becomes possible to interpret the changes in the retinal image as indicating the approach of a projectile. This interpretation makes explicit the probable cause of the image change, and catching behaviour can be controlled accordingly.

The lens of an eye focusses light rays so that they form a two-dimensional image. The intensity of a ray from some surface depends on the intensity of the illuminance of the surface, the orientation of the surface to the direction of illumination and the reflectance of the surface. Thus the intensity of light at a point in the image only partly relates to the character of the surface, not at all to the distance of the surface. The light rays enter the eyes after being repeatedly reflected off surfaces in a three-dimensional space. The intensity, wavelength and direction (with respect to the eye) of each ray is preserved explicitly in the image, but the distance over which it has travelled is only implicit in the spatial distribution of ray intensities.

Vision is the process which recovers these properties of the scene. Without help, vision is impossible, just as it is impossible to deduce from the datum:

$$x + 2x^2 + y^3 = 1$$

what the value of x is. If it is known, that y is always very small, then a tentative solution for the value of x may be obtained:

$$x + 2x^2 + 0 = 1 \ (y \langle\langle 1)$$
$$x = 1/2 \text{ or } -1$$

General knowledge about y leads to a good approximation for x. Similarly, vision depends on general knowledge about light sources and their effects on typical scenes, if it is to produce an approximate description of the three dimensional shapes and disposition of bodies in the scene or environment. Even then, the meaning and significance of each body in the scene depends on the state and needs of the observer. A chair is suitable for sitting upon both because it offers a stable, knee-height, flat surface of appropriate size and because it can be recognised as belonging to the psychological category of chairs. It is also useful for stacking papers on.

The process of categorisation is also not simple. The **visual problem** is that the degrees of freedom afforded by three-dimensional space make it unlikely that the same body will ever be imaged with exactly the same projection. The **cognitive problem** is that the same physical body can be a number of alternative objects of processing, that is, meanings to the perceiver. Consider a tree in a garden. This is a physical body with a particular shape and place in the scene. The type of behaviour that we direct towards this body determines the type of object it becomes. If we are just walking around the garden it is an obstacle to be avoided; if we are looking for something to eat then it is not an obstacle but a tree with fruit-bearing branches. The body can be recognised as an obstacle or a mulberry tree; the body can belong to the wide category of obstacles or the narrow category of mulberry trees or many other categories.

At some level of abstraction the process of categorisation or recognition involves the matching of an input data representation that might be incomplete or partial against a representation of the criteria defining a category. Sometimes this matching is trivial as when we recognise a triangle by the presence of three angles, each connected by a straight line to each of the other two. This representation of a triangle is necessary for defining the category. Non-trivial cases usually involve partial representations in which case the category definition will have some necessary components, some probable components, some admissible components, and some inadmissible components. A flexible representation of a face might have: as a necessary component, ovoid outline; as probable components, one or two eyes, one mouth, one nose; as admissible components, a moustache, and one or more scars; as inadmissible components, three eyes, a thumb etc.

Since each of the components (eye, nose etc) in such a partial representation is itself a label describing another representation, it is necessary to invoke the concept of a grammar to control the construction of arbitrary categories. The alphabet upon which the grammar acts will ultimately be based on the primitives that represent the intrinsic scene characteristics.

PART 1: ARCHITECTURE OF THE VISION PROBLEM

There is an architectural pattern to vision, not as a system, but as a process or problem. All visual processes start with a **task** and a **stimulus**. The stimulus has to be **processed** to remove unwanted data and to make the desired data accessible or explicit. But this is just the first step since the outcome of processing a signal is also just a signal which has to be **analyzed** and measured to find meaningful patterns in the signal and to make an initial description of the image features found. These descriptions of the image need to be **interpreted** as being caused by surfaces and bodies in the scene. Finally the process needs to be **controlled**.

These are logically different types of operation; they could each perhaps be modelled by the same linear or recursive computer program or mathematical mapping. They could possibly all be implemented in one nerve cell. We are not concerned with the modularity of vision in terms of its hardware anatomy but as it might be understood. Therefore, research must necessarily involve investigations at several of these different logical levels. It would not be meaningful to consider corner detection for an example, without asking what the visual projection of corners and occlusions actually were, and what the visual system might use corners for.

However the intellect tends to be confined by frameworks of this type. Recent history in vision research (for which the authors acknowledge their share of the blame) illustrates this tendency. The legacy of the late David Marr is a framework comprising "Primal Sketch"; "2.5D Sketch"; "viewer-centred co-ordinate systems" and "object-centred co-ordinate systems". Primal sketch has come to mean edge-detection and motion-detection; 2.5D sketch has come to mean stereopsis, optic flow and motion parallax. The reified concept of "Primal Sketch" has led to a baffling array of edge detectors all starting with the assumption, implied by Marr, that the interesting parts of images are always (deformed) discontinuities in luminance. This assumption creates the correspondence problem for stereoscopic algorithms within the 2.5D sketch of how to match corresponding edge elements in the two binocular images. Another consequence of the edge assumption has been that motion research has concentrated on the aperture problem: the direction of motion of a surface is not recoverable from the motion of any one edge point in the image of that surface (Hildreth, 1984).

Could different, less troublesome primitives be used? The trouble with edge points is that they are essentially one dimensional; if truly two-dimensional primitives were used these problems would be less severe. The point is that a great deal of work inspired by Marr's framework, was also confined by the framework.

The solution to these pragmatic problems is mostly political. Diversity of approach is the only real sign of intellectual health and must always be encouraged.

With these strictures in mind we now examine the six facets of understanding. In each case we identify the fundamental conceptual problems and then ask what knowledge is lacking.

1. Visual Tasks

Is it possible to list all the biological functions and requirements of vision? For a protozoan this would not be difficult. For a fly this has proved, at least in part, to be practical. For humans, it is an open question at present whether this will be possible. The human brain may be so opportunistic that vision is continually being turned to new tasks such as orientation in conditions of weightlessness.

The idea of general purpose vision is common. What it implies is unclear. It might mean that vision makes all scene and illumination information available all the time so that any arbitrary task can be accomplished. This is plainly far from the truth. Try counting the lines of text on this page rapidly but without pointing at them: this is a perfectly reasonable task, but you will find it far from easy to do.

It is necessary to construct a generic set of visual tasks which could be taken as encompassing the main functions and uses of vision. Once such a set has been created, the next step will be to define the type of information that each task required (e.g. Lee, 1980). The aim would be to devise a basic set of visual representations that are minimal for human vision.

2. The Stimulus

A comprehensive understanding of vision will call upon a general description of the visual stimulus. It is universally acknowledged that the set of all possible 2D images of real or feasible 3D scenes is extremely large, but also extremely small with respect to the set of all possible images (e.g. Srinivasan et al., 1982). It is also accepted that the partition into meaningful and nonsense images concerns pattern, structure and regularity. Just what pattern, structure and regularity is not known.

The defining characteristics of meaningful images are usually expressed as constraints on images that derive from the behaviour of matter and forces in 3D space. We need to know what these constraints are, how generally they hold, and both the circumstances in which they do not hold and the consequences of these failures.

Many of the constraints are precisely determined by the cosine and inverse square laws of illumination. Others are statistically determined by the manner in which natural surfaces are created, such as the carpet of leaves under a tree in autumn. It would be very useful to know what texture patterns natural forces tend to produce. When this is known a rigourous specification of texture gradients and discontinuities will follow with little effort. Fractals may be very relevant (Mandelbrot, 1982; Pentland, 1984).

3.Visual Processing

The visual image has an extremely high information content. Much of the explicit information is irrelevant because it is related to the conditions of illumination. Processing the image is necessary to reveal the information that is pertinent to scene characteristics. For example the mean luminance, due entirely to the number, disposition and intensity of light sources, can be removed by differentiating the image. Differentiating preserves only the differences in surface luminance. If two surfaces of reflectance R_1 and R_2 are adjacent and have the same illuminance, I, then preceding the differencing by a logarithmic transformation of the image will result in a measure of their reflectance ratio because:

$$\log (IR_1) - \log (IR_2) = \log (IR_1/IR_2) = \log (R_1/R_2)$$

Processing an image does not change the domain. An image is drawn from the domain of real valued 2D functions, R2, and so is a processed image.

Processing an image can be done for two reasons: to reveal the scene geometrical structure (where occluding boundaries lie, what 3D slope the intervening surfaces have) and also to reveal the surface characteristics such as colour and texture. The visual processing involved in revealing surface characteristics has received some recent attention (e.g., Ninio and Mizraji, 1984; Nothdurft, 1985; Glünder, 1986; Sagi and Julesz, 1987). The use of oriented or elongated filters has only received scant study, and yet the psychophysics and physiology of vision indicate their presence in human vision (Robson, 1983). It is possible that when the outputs of oriented filters are combined appropriately they may reveal a wide range of texture discontinuities.

The use of visual processing techniques to reveal motion and image change deserves continued study (Lupp, Hauske and Wolf, 1978; Roufs and Blommaert, 1981; Moulden, Renshaw and Mather, 1984). Most studies of motion have been based on discrete quantization of time into video frames. Human vision is continuous in time. This must be taken into account.

The possibility of non-trivial 2D primitives, such as corners and line intersections (Watt, 1986) should be explored further. There is considerable interest in 2D attributes of lines and edges, such as curvature (Watt and Andrews, 1982; Ferraro and Foster, 1986).

4. Analysis and Physical Measurement

Once the information in an image that is characteristic of the scene has been made more accessible by processing, it is necessary to examine the image and create a description of the image structure. This description will obviously need to be rich so that scene properties that are not explicit in images can be interpreted. The description must also use suitable primitives to suit the interpretation process. An example of this type of issue is provided by Rentschler (Rentschler and Treutwein, 1985; Caelli, Hübner and Rentschler, 1986).

In a general sense there are conceptual difficulties. The significance of measurements such as of the curvature of a line needs proper logical analysis. In this context the notion of error-correcting mappings and metrics may be central (Andrews, 1964). This work has been extended by Watt (1987, 1988).

A conceptual problem concerns the nature of the description that is produced. In machine vision systems it is general to use vector fields, functions, and maps. So for example local motions in an image are represented by a dense field or map of vectors; the shape of a closed curve is represented as a curvature function. Whilst this may often be convenient or at least acceptable, how could it be used to describe a patch of texture? A map or function is quite inappropriate, and an alternative must be found.

Another issue that will become increasingly important concerns how the output of different filters can be combined. In machine vision systems, at present, it is often feasible to manage with only one filter because of the restricted scope of images. The move towards general purpose vision systems will make the use of more than one size of filter necessary and the problem of how to combine their outputs will be paramount (e.g. Watt and Morgan, 1985; Koenderink, 1984b).

5. Interpretation and Recognition

The scene characteristics in images have to be interpreted in terms of scene structure. For example, the local motions of edge bits in an image cannot be directionally specified to less than 180 degrees (the aperture problem). However it is possible to take all the motions of edge bits around a closed contour and infer the motion of the body that is responsible (Hildreth, 1984). Typically the interpretation stage involves the combination of various different image measures each from widespread loci in the image. These are not generally suited to local neighbourhood operations and limited-connection parallel processing.

One important aspect of the interpretation problem is the combination of information from different cues to a particular scene property, e.g. motion parallax, binocular disparity, shading and occlusion information for depth. Some work has been done in this area (e.g. Rogers and Collett, 1985). The combination of information from different sense modalities is important in interpretation as well.

Many of the interpretation problems rely on the nature of the image descriptions available. The two classic interpretation problems, namely the aperture problem of motion just referred to, and the correspondence problem of stereopsis which concerns matching two disparate images, are both severe if the basic primitive is an edge bit or zero-crossing. If the basic primitive is a corner or curved line, these problems may become less severe. Beyond this there is the question of whether stereoscopic disparity or gradients or curvatures of disparity should be or are represented. Disparity curvatures may be especially suitable because they remain invariant with viewing distance. Rogers (1986) has psychophysical evidence in favour of disparity curvature primitives.

The interpretation problem also applies to the visual understanding of surface shape/volumetric representation, to colour and lightness, and to the visual representation of the geometry and topology of spatial relations between items in the scene.

The issues of visual recognition and categorisation are, of course, specific instances of the general interpretation paradigm. Recognition is a complex behaviour which operates at many levels. Take the case of a view of someone's face. This single image can be recognized as a face; a male or female face; a face from a particular racial group; a young or old face; a happy or sad face; a familiar or unfamiliar face; the face of a particular individual. It is clearly not the case that there is some process which can be described as "object recognition" which assigns a representation to an input thereby achieving recognition. The way in which something is recognized depends on what behaviour is being undertaken at the time and the reasons for seeking a particular recognition (cf. Bruce and Young, 1986 for a review).

To date there has been very little examination of the conceptual structure of the interpretation operations beyond the two classic cases. This area is bound to be at the centre of robotics applications.

6. Control

In considering the control of visual processes, we must return to the starting point: tasks. Vision is purposeful but not single-minded. The type of visual representation desired depends upon the task that is to be undertaken. This implies either universality or control. The latter is much the more plausible as has been discussed. This leads to the issue of top-down control of vision, such as is implied by the "perceptual hypotheses" ideas of Gregory (1980).

This is a topic of which we are almost totally ignorant. It will be difficult to make real progress until the dynamics of the various visual operations are understood (Weisstein and Wong, 1986). What operations require iteration, even in parallel machinery and therefore are both slow and variable (because the number of iterations is not fixed)? What is the relationship between these critical operations and the dynamics of visual image change?

PART 2: THE INDIVIDUAL APPROACHES

There are four distinct approaches presently involved in the understanding of vision: computational theory, computational modelling, experimental psychology and physiology. Physiology is beyond the scope of this paper, (qv. Neuroscience paper by Orban, Volume 4). Briefly, there is one major obstacle preventing the unification of psychophysics and physiology. Psychophysics is useful for discovering the mathematical models or the algorithms for visual mechanisms. At present there is no theory of how such models should be implemented in neural tissue, although the results of research into parallel distributed processing may provide such a theory.

In this section we address the issue of what is lacking in each approach that might be important for an overall study of vision. It should be borne in mind that the views are intentionally personal.

1. Computational Theory

Computational theory is concerned with examining the information requirements of specific tasks and discovering ways of satisfying these requirements (Marr, 1976). Gibson's (1966) analysis of optic flow is an example of this type of work. Usually in perception, the image signal alone does not provide sufficient information to accomplish a task and has to be augmented with a priori knowledge of scene and image constraints. In general, future work in computational theory will require the development of new mathematical techniques or at least the adaptation of existing techniques.

The usual physical approach to manifolds (surfaces) and spaces involves differential geometry and differential topology (Koenderink, 1984a). These may be useful for some shapes, but are however quite inappropriate for analysing the shape of a tree for example, unless modified (Koenderink & Van Doorn 1986). Another important example is the development of fuzzy set theory as a tool for specifying the task of recognition (Foster, 1979).

2. Computational Modelling

If computational theory is the engineer's specification of the required performance of a machine, then computational modelling is about how such a machine could be made and how its various parts will work. Modelling involves examination of potential algorithms for recovering information in the input data and for using that recovered information to perform tasks. It also involves consideration of available machinery and its computing potential.

It is quite clear that more research is needed at this level in vision. The visual system uses massively parallel computational techniques at its front end and most machine vision systems start with processes that rely on local neighbourhood operations which are eminently suitable for implementation on parallel machinery. Many of the interpretive stages of vision however require operations that do not have an exclusively local support and there is scant understanding of the behaviour of the types of machinery that could be used to implement these stages.

Another area needing investigation concerns the control and performance characteristics of iterative processes such as constraint relaxation. There are potentially complex interactions between timing and control requirements on the one hand and dynamic memory usage on the other. More generally, the control, sequencing and timing of processes which are inherently slow but not deterministically (i.e. when speed depends on image complexity) will need to be examined. This is particularly true of processes that can proceed asynchronously across the visual field. The work of Ullman (1984) on visual routines and Duff (1986) on neighbourhood operations are good examples of what can be achieved by examining how to go about computing certain image properties.

3. Experimental Psychology

Traditionally there have been two distinct disciplines within the general area of behavioural studies of vision: psychophysics and human information processing. Each has viewed the other with the suspicion of being "too low-level" or "too high-level". These categories are absurd. There are, however significant differences in the type of result that is obtained and interpretation that is possible.

At a superficial level, psychophysics measures sensitivities (thresholds) and human information processing measures reaction times. The difference is deeper than this. Reaction times should be a good measure of the dynamic and temporal aspects of visual processing. Sensitivities should be a good measure of the information available. In practice, it is more often the case that sensitivities lead to quantitative conclusions about the algorithms, whereas reaction times only lead to binary decisions between different hypotheses.

3a. Psychophysics

Psychophysics is the objective study of the physical characteristics of vision. Psychophysicists have well established methods for measuring the differential

sensitivity of the visual system to changes in stimulation. These are generally termed "thresholds", but the word is very misleading, because it implies a fixed boundary. There also exist techniques for measuring the **bias** of the visual system. Suppose we take an upright rectangle and ask a subject to decide whether the height is greater or less than the width. We repeat this several times for each of a range of different heights, some smaller and some larger than the width. By collecting the proportion of "greater than" judgements at each height value, we can assess how rapidly the subject's response switches from "greater than" to "less than": the steeper the change the more sensitive the visual system. The height at which the observer will respond "greater than" on 50% of all occasions corresponds to the bias of the visual system. If it is exactly the same as the width of the box, then the observer has a zero bias and the point of subjective equality is equal to the point of objective equality. It is often assumed that psychophysics only measures the conscious experience of vision. This is most unlikely to be true. Folklore amongst psychophysicists holds that the least variable data is obtained when subjects are alert but not concentrating exclusively on the task. Subjects report that they were guessing near threshold, but the data show that their "guesses" are often very reliable. The implication is that unconscious information is being used.

Sensitivity is inversely proportional to the standard deviation of the subject's errors. This makes it a powerful measure, because it is known from the axioms of statistics that standard deviations sum quadratically when independent. In other words, variance is a linear quantity with respect to the normal operations of algebra, and more particularly adds under convolution. The theory of how to analyze sensitivities is therefore well developed and rests on a small number of unexceptional assumptions.

The greatest need in the area of psychophysics is for more sophisticated paradigms and greater precision in measurement techniques. For example, if one wishes to study the time course of a visual process it is customary to measure the effects of exposure duration on sensitivity and bias. This is clearly simplistic because the receptors in the eye have a considerable persistence which means that the effective visual duration is not the same as the physical duration. The normal solution is to blank out the stimulus using a masking pattern but in so doing, the stimulus has been changed as has the task executed by the visual system, which has no reason to "know" about masks.

3b. Human Information Processing

Within the area of cognitive psychology, there is an approach which is distinct from the computational and the psychophysical disciplines. This approach is called human information processing, and its practitioners tend to see their theories and experiments as examining the overall structure or architecture of vision in terms of the **flow of information**. Typical issues considered are: whether or not high level, declarative knowledge can influence visual processing; whether the selection of the objects of vision is made early or late in processing; and whether prior processing of a stimulus, even if unconscious, can influence the subsequent processing.

Whilst the information processing approach is not invalid, at least within its own philosophy, many of its central constructs such as "visual attention", "consciousness", "objects", "priming" do not map at all onto computational and psychophysical work. Many of these constructs, which appear to be based originally on intuition and introspection, do not appear to have relevance for a computational or psychophysical understanding of vision. This approach is nevertheless a useful one, and its concern with the different levels of information processing will be of value to the understanding of vision. This concern is currently being turned to the properties of parallel distributed processing networks.

The typical measure made in an experiment belonging to this field is a reaction time. It is not simple to analyze distributions of reaction times. Many authors only report the mean or median, without a measure of dispersion except in a test of significance. Mean or median reaction times cannot be expected to sum in any simple analytic fashion, and they are often heavily constrained by serial response dependencies. At present these problems effectively prevent the type of quantitative analysis of reaction time data that might lead to a computational or algorithmic understanding of the mechanism involved.

3c. Future Combined Studies

It is becoming clear that the visual system has a variable state, depending on what task is being undertaken (e.g., Weisstein and Wong, 1986). It is perhaps more realistic at present to consider the existence of many "visual systems" each tailored to a particular task. These different visual systems could be from different parts of the visual field, so that the periphery of the visual image is treated differently from the centre. They could also be from the same part of the visual field, but subserving different tasks such as walking, identifying trees etc. It would be very interesting to know more about the information available to the different visual systems.

The type of experiment that would be useful to conduct might be like this. Subjects are asked to reach out and touch the end of a small rod on the table in front of them. Certain places in the trajectory traced out by their finger tip will be the loci of changes in movement due to visual feedback. From a visual point of view the question that follows is what stimulus variables affect the precision of the trajectory, particularly at such places and by what amounts. How does a +2 Dioptre defocus of the eye affect performance, for example? Does this depend on whether the subjects are also monitoring the scene for the appearance of a red light?

PART 3: INTER-DISCIPLINARY CO-OPERATION

Research into human vision is currently active and very productive. Scientists from various disciplines, notably astronomy, engineering, physics, physiology and experimental psychology have all contributed their own perspective sa to the nature of the problem and skills for its study. To these we may add the emerging fields of artificial intelligence, cognitive psychology, computer science, medical physics, and robotics. Each discipline adds its own characteristic viewpoint and understanding to the subject of perception, but often with insufficient knowledge of the other approaches and their methods and limitations. Vision research has one of the longest traditions of cross-disciplinary interaction amongst the cognitive sciences and some of the lessons learned will be instructive to other areas of cognitive science.

One major obstacle to progress is the incomplete appreciation of the strengths and weaknesses of the different disciplines and the almost total absence of any detailed examination of the logical links involved. There has long been an appreciation of the need for a formal linking hypothesis before psychophysics can be related to the behaviour of single cells in the visual pathway and vice versa, but few specific proposals. In their absence, rather restrictive views of the relationship between psychophysics and physiology have grown informally. The exceptions are the two well articulated proposals by Barlow, (1972) and Teller, (1984). The impact of these papers has been surprisingly slight and more study is needed.

Collaboration between human vision and machine vision researchers is a most exciting prospect. The human visual sense provides both an existence proof for the possibility of achieving certain tasks such as artefact manipulation or navigation with visual information, and the enticing possibility of a general purpose visual system. This is a much respected concept in machine vision, but one which to date has proved elusive. Human vision research needs the existence of a thriving machine vision enquiry to provide the techniques for a critical test of theory. Although many aspects of human vision are undoubtedly amenable to a purely intellectual understanding, the synthesis of many parts will require simulations of vision to be run in the presence of real operating difficulties such as noise, image jitter and distortion.

Human vision research and machine vision research also encourage and stimulate each other. It is not grossly misleading to say that much of the effort expended in machine vision has been based primarily on an intuitive and introspective understanding of what people can see. The more that is objectively known about human vision, the more valid it will be as an inspiration to machine vision. Similarly research into human vision draws continually on the experience of machine vision systems. Researchers learn new ways of understanding established or proposed mechanisms; they discover that some putative mechanisms would be counterproductive to the assumed goals of vision; most importantly they learn that there are fundamental limitations on the capacity of any device and fundamental problems of information processing that must be solved.

It takes a sympathetic, trained eye to see through the vast literature of psychophysics and psychology to the incontrovertible facts, the well tested and supported hypotheses as opposed to the wild speculation. experimental psychologists allow a generous public interpretation of their experiments that may mislead the unwary. It is also true that characteristic skills are required for orientation to the machine vision literature, much of which employs an increasingly esoteric language. Training in both areas will be needed to bridge these gaps.

REFERENCES

Andrews, D.P. (1964) Error-correcting perceptual mechanisms. *Quarterly Journal of Experimental Psychology, 16,* 104-115.

Barlow, H.B. (1972) Single units and sensation: a neuron doctrine for perceptual psychology? *Perception, 1,* 371-394.

Bruce, V. & Young, A. (1986) Understanding Face Recognition. *British Journal of Psychology, 77,* 305-327.

Caelli, T., Hübner, M. & Rentschler, J. (1986) On the discrimination of micropatterns and textures. *Human Neurobiology, 5,* 129-136.

Duff, M.J.B. (1986) Complexity. In M.J.B. Duff (ed) *Intermediate-Level Image Processing.* Academic Press.

Ferraro, M. & Foster, D.H. (1986) Discrete and continuous modes of curved-line discrimination controlled by effective stimulus duration. *Spatial Vision, 1,* 219-230.

Foster, D.H. (1979) Fuzzy topological groups. *Journal of Mathematical Analysis and Applications, 67,* 549-564.

Gibson, J.J. (1966) *The Senses Considered as Perceptual systems.* Boston. Mass.

Glünder, H. (1986) Neural Comptation of Inner Geonmetric Pattern Relations. *Biological Cybernetics, 55,* 239-251.

Gregory, R.L. (1980) Perceptions as hypotheses. *Philosophical Transactions of the Royal Society London, B290,* 181-197.

Hildreth, E.C. (1984) Computations Underlying the Measurement of Visual Motion. *Artificial Intelligence, 23,* 309-354.

Koenderink, J. (1984a) What does the occluding contour tell us about solid shape? *Perception, 13,* 321-330.

Koenderink, J.J. (1984b) The structure of images. *Biological Cybernetics, 50,* 363-370.

Koenderink, J.J. and van Doorn, A.J. (1986) Dynamic Shape. *Biological Cybernetics, 53,* 383-396.

Lee, D. (1980) The Optic Flow Field: the foundation of vision. *Philosophical Transactions of the Royal Society London. B290,* 169-179.

Lupp, U., Hauske, G. & Wolf, W. (1978) Different systems of the visual detection of high and low spatial frequencies. *Photographic Science and Engineering, 22,* 80-84.

Mandelbrot, B.B. (1982) *The Fractal Geometry of Nature.* Freeman, San Francisco.

Marr, D.C. (1976). *Vision.* Freeman, San Francisco.

Marr, D.C. (1982) *Vision.* W.H. Freeman, San Francisco.

Mather, G. (1984) Luminance change generates apparent movement: implications for models of directional specificity on the human visual system. *Vision Res., 24,* 1399-1405.

Moulden, B., Renshaw, J., Mather, G. (1984) Two channels for flicker in the human visual system. *Perception, 13,* 387-400.

Ninio, J. & Mizraji, E. (1985) Errors in the stereoscopic separation of surfaces represented with regular textures. *Perception, 14,* 315-328.

Nothdurft, H.C. (1985) Discrimination of higher-order textures. *Perception, 14,* 539-543.

Pentland, A. (1984) Fractal-based description of natural scenes. *IEEE PAMI, 6,* 661-665.

Rentschler, I. and Treutwein, B. (1985) Loss of spatial phase relationships in extrafoveal vision. *Nature, 313,* 308-310.

Robson, J.R. (1983) Frequency domain visual processing. In *Physical and Biological Processing of Images.* O. Braddick and A.Sleigh (Eds.). Springer Verlag, Berlin.

Rogers, B.J. (1986) Perception of surface curvature from disparity and motion parallax cues. *Investigative Ophthalmology & Visual Science, Suppl. 27.*

Rogers, B. & Collett, T. (1985) Rigidity and perceived depth in surfaces specified by disparity and parallax cues. *Investigative Ophthalmology & Visual Science, Suppl. 26.*

Roufs, J.A.J. & Blommaert, F.J.J. (1981) Temporal impulse and step responses of the human eye obtained psychophysically by means of a drift-correcting perturbation technique. *Vision Research,*

21, 1203-1221.

Sagi, D. and Julesz, B. (1987) Short-range limitation on detection of feature differences. *Spatial Vision*, 2, 39-50.

Srinivasan, M.V., Laughlin, S.B., & Dubs, A. (1982) Predictive coding: a fresh view of inhibition in the retina. *Proceedings of the Royal Society London, B216*, 427-459.

Teller, D.Y. (1984) Linking propositions. *Vision Research, 24*, 1233-1246.

Ullman, S. (1984) Visual Routines. *Cognition, 18*, 97-159.

Watt, R.J. (1986). Feature based image segmentation in human vision. *Spatial Vision, 1*, 243–256.

Watt, R.J. (1987) An outline of the primal sketch in human vision. *Pattern Recognition Letters, 5*, 139-150.

Watt, R.J. (1988) *Visual Processing: Computational, Psychophysical and Cognitive Research. L.E.A.*, (London).

Watt R.J. & Andrews. D.P. (1982) Contour Curvature Analysis: Hyperacuities in the discrimination of defailed shape. *Vision Research, 22*, 449-460.

Watt, R.J. & Morgan, M.J. (1985) A theory of the primitive spatial code in human vision. *Vision Research, 25*, 1661-1674.

Weisstein N. & Wong. E (1986). Figure-ground organization and the spatial and temporal responses of the visual system. In *Pattern Recognition by Humans and Machines* E.C. Schwab and H.C. Nusbaum (Eds.). Academic Press, Orlando.

CHAPTER 3

AUDITORY PREPROCESSING AND RECOGNITION OF SPEECH

Roy D. Patterson and Anne Cutler

MRC Applied Psychology Unit,
15 Chaucer Road,
Cambridge CB2 2EF ,
England

INTRODUCTION

For some time now, research on automatic speech recognition (ASR) has been largely concerned with what might be called the signal processing approach, in which the recognition of speech by machines was viewed as an information processing problem, quite distinct from the problem of how humans recognise speech. The signal-processing approach has had considerable success in the sense that it has produced a succession of special purpose devices that can recognise speech provided the vocabulary and the number of speakers is limited. It has not, however, led to the development of a general purpose ASR machine that can handle continuous speech from an arbitrary group of speakers using the vocabulary typical of normal conversation. It is also the case that the performance of current systems falls away rapidly when they are required to operate in noisy or reverberant environments.

The question then arises as to how best to proceed in the pursuit of the general purpose ASR machine. Some speech scientists argue that we should continue with the signal processing approach; that the quickest and surest route to the general machine is to refine the existing techniques and algorithms. An excellent review of the signal processing approach is presented in Bristow (1986). Others argue that current systems

23

have inherent limitations that cannot be overcome within the signal processing framework, and that we must begin again with new concepts and processes. A portion of the latter group feel that the best way to proceed is to determine how humans process speech sounds and to develop a functional model of the human hearing and speech systems, the only speech recogniser with proven ability. An ASR machine which divides the problem up into the same sub-processes as the human brain, which provides some equivalent of the processing observed at each stage, and which performs the transformations in the same order, seems more likely to be successful than one which pays less attention to the human solution. This is the cognitive psychology approach, in contrast to the signal processing approach, and it is this approach that is the topic of the current chapter.

The psychological approach has the advantage of face validity; in the longer term it is bound to succeed. The problem is that we do not currently understand human speech processing well enough to assemble a complete functional model of the system, and even if we did, it would be too large to serve as the basis for a commercial ASR machine at this point in time. The purpose of this chapter, however, is not to explain how the psychological approach can solve all of the problems of speech recognition either now or in the near future. Rather its purpose is to point to the limitations of the signal-processing approach that have led to the re-emergence of the psychological direction in speech recognition, and to highlight some of the advances achieved by and projected for the psychological approach.

It is important to note that we are making the distinction between the signal-processing approach and the cognitive-psychology approach primarily in order to delimit the topic of this chapter. Like most dichotomies, it is not a hard and fast distinction. Furthermore, it is undoubtedly the case that both approaches will play a role in the development of ASR machines, along with others that do not even appear in the chapter. In making the distinction we simply intend to focus attention on a new direction in speech research and to indicate the origins and predilections of the scientists involved. The chapter is also restricted in terms of the portion of the speech problem with which it is concerned. It covers the processing of speech from the initial reception of an acoustic signal by the peripheral auditory system to the location in memory of a corresponding stored representation. It does not cover any higher-level processing such as the selection between alternative meanings for a homophone, contextual facilitation effects, syntactic evaluation, or integration into semantic context.

The research we will summarise falls into three parts: auditory perception which has traditionally been the province of psychoacousticians, word recognition which has traditionally been studied by psycholinguists, and the interface between the two which is essentially a new area of research. Parts 1 and 2 of this chapter outline the current research issues in auditory perception and word recognition, respectively. The description of the interface is deferred until Part 3, despite its logical position between hearing and speech, because it is qualitatively different. Whereas auditory perception and word recognition are established research areas that can be reviewed in a straightforward way, interfacing models of hearing and speech is a new speculative venture which is currently characterised by small scale demonstrations of promising leads rather than proven large scale systems. A brief description of the interface problem is presented in the next subsection of the Introduction. The final subsection presents an extended example of one of the problems with the signal-processing approach to illustrate the motivation for returning to auditory models as preprocessors for auditory speech recognition.

A. Interfacing Auditory Models with Speech Models

Although speech sounds are a subset of auditory perceptions, there has been surprisingly little interaction between psychoacousticians and psycholinguists over the years. One of the main problems is that the two groups work with very different representations of sounds; the psychoacousticians represent speech, like other sounds, as arrays of filtered waveforms, whereas psycholinguists have tended to use phonetic codes, or some other discrete representation of sounds. The auditory models are massively parallel with from 30 to 300 channels, the parallelism continues through a number of auditory processing stages, and the reduction to a stream of auditory sensations occurs late in the system if it occurs at all. Speech models, in contrast, typically begin with relatively simple spectral analyses and reduce the parallel output of the spectral analysis to a serial string of speech features as early in the system as possible. Thus, the two types of model have different internal representations, involving vastly different data rates, throughout the majority of the processing stages, and it has not been possible to assemble an integrated model in which the output of an auditory front-end constructed by a psychoacoustician is used as the input to a speech processor constructed by a psycholinguist.

The current chapter provides an unfortunate example of the problem of differing internal representations. The first and second parts were written by a psychoacoustician and a psycholinguist, respectively, and despite our efforts to integrate them, the continuity of the chapter is severely disrupted by the differences in the representations used in the two parts. The contrast is useful, however, insofar as it shows the enormity of the speech recognition problem when one attempts to assemble a complete cognitive psychological representation of the process.

Recently, the situation has begun to change, and in an interesting way. Psychoacousticians and speech scientists with a psychological orientation have begun developing spectro-temporal auditory models to simulate the neural firing patterns produced in the auditory system by complex sounds like speech and music. At the same time, speech scientists, in conjunction with psycholinguists, have been developing models that attempt to derive the phonetic representation from the auditory data stream rather than taking it as given. As a result, there is now considerable interest in establishing common representations and determining where and how the reduction from a high-data-rate parallel system to a low-data-rate serial system occurs. Part 3 of the chapter outlines three approaches currently used to reduce the spectral representation of speech to phonology or words, and considers how each might be expanded to accommodate the high data rates flowing from spectro-temporal auditory models.

B. The Spectrogram and the Auditory Filter Bank

Prior to about 1950, hearing and speech were more closely related sciences in the sense that researchers who worked on one very often worked on the other. Much of the work on hearing was done with the explicit intention of developing a better understanding of speech perception and both groups took a basically psychological approach. About this time, however, many psychoacousticians turned away from speech and began to try and relate auditory perception to more peripheral, rather than more central, processes. Using linear systems analysis and signal detection theory, they built spectral models of masking and discrimination that related human perception to the frequency analysis performed by the basilar membrane. For simplicity, the models tended to concentrate on the peripheral activity produced by stationary sinusoids presented on their own or in noise.

Unfortunately, such models are of limited use to speech scientists trying to determine the critical auditory features required to distinguish, say, [e] from [a]. There were also practical constraints on the amount of computation that could be allocated to the front-end processor. For these and other reasons, many speech groups chose, effectively, to finesse the problem of auditory analysis by assuming that the spectrogram would serve as a sufficient front-end processor for speech stimuli.

1. The Spectrogram

A spectrogram of the word "past" spoken by an English Canadian is shown in Figure 1a; the vertical and horizontal dimensions are frequency and time, respectively. The central section of the figure with the vertical striations represents the vowel [ae]. vowels are voiced sounds, that is, they are quasi-periodic, and it is this property that generates the temporal regularity in the spectrogram. In contrast, there is an irregular patch of high frequency energy just after the vowel, which represents the [s]. It is an unvoiced speech sound (a burst of noise) and so there is a lack of temporal regularity in this region of the spectrogram. The dark horizontal bands in the vowel show concentrations of energy known as formants. In ASR, the position and trajectory of the formants are used to identify vowels. Recognition machines based on this kind of representation have had considerable success. They have the advantage of being relatively inexpensive and some of them operate in real time. As noted earlier however, there remains considerable room for improvement as performance is poor in noisy or reverberant environments.

The primary problem with the spectrogram is that it simply does not have sufficient resolution. It enables one to detect the presence of formants and to track their motion, but it does not have the resolution required to reveal the shapes of the formants within the pitch period, information that might be expected to assist with speaker identification and speaker adaptation. As a result it is not a satisfactory substitute for auditory analysis.

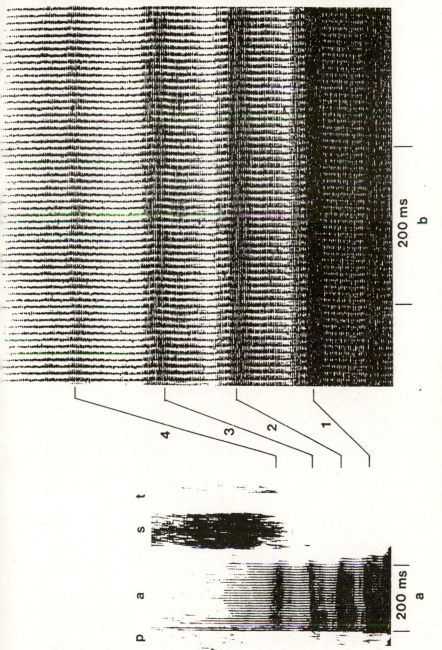

FIG. 3.1   Spectrograms of (a) the word "past" and (b) an enlargement of a sustained version of the vowel in "past". The abscissa is time, the ordinate is linear frequency, and the enlargement factor is 2.4. Note that the graininess of the enlargement is due to the resolution of the original spectrogram, and that the shapes of the formants are not apparent in this representation.

An enlargement of a sustained section of the vowel [ae] is presented in Figure 1b to show that the resolution problem is not simply a matter of the overall size of the spectrogram. The blurry edges of the smallest features show that we have reached the limits of the resolution of this analysis method. The enlargement shows that the energy in the formant track is not evenly distributed throughout the pitch period, and this indicates that more formant information is available at higher levels of magnification, but the shape of the formant within the pitch period does not exist in this representation.

It is also the case that the spectrogram is incompatible with both psychoacoustic and physiological representations of the auditory periphery, and so its use in speech research had the effect of increasing the gap between the speech and hearing communities in the 1950s and 1960s. With regard to psychoacoustics, the problem is that the spectrogram is a very poor predictor of auditory masking. The primary determinant of auditory masking is the bandwidth of the auditory filter which in normal adults increases from around 70 Hz at the low end of the speech range to around 700 Hz at the high end of the speech range. The spectrogram is like an auditory filterbank in which all of the filters have the same bandwidth. In the standard spectrogram, like that of Figure 1, the filter has a bandwidth of 300 Hz. As a result, the spectrogram over-estimates auditory masking at low frequencies and under-estimates it at high frequencies, to a degree that is simply unacceptable to psychoacousticians. With regard to auditory physiology, the problem with the spectrogram is that it integrates over too long a time, and so smears out the details of basilar membrane motion. As a result, it precludes any physiological model involving phase locking and any attempt to develop a realistic model of the firing patterns observed in the auditory nerve. Thus, the spectrogram is completely unacceptable to auditory physiologists as a representation of peripheral spectral analysis.

2. The Auditory Filter Bank

The separation between hearing and speech research persisted until about ten years ago, at which point the availability of more powerful computers made it possible to consider assembling full scale simulations of peripheral auditory processing (Young and Sachs, 1979; Dolmazon, 1982; Delgutte, 1980). At about the same time, psychoacousticians began to come to grips with the problems posed for their models by complex sounds (Yost and Watson, 1987), and speech scientists became concerned with the fidelity of their representations of speech sounds (Lyon, 1984; Schofield, 1985; Seneff, 1984). The net result is that there is a new common ground for hearing and speech research in the form of elaborate spectro-temporal auditory models, whose purpose is to characterise the patterns of information produced by complex sounds in the auditory nerve, and to process the patterns into a stream of auditory features and speech phonology (Beet, Moore and Tomlinson, 1986; Cooke, 1986; Gardner and Uppal, 1986; Ghitza, 1986; Hunt & Lefebvre, 1987; Patterson, 1987a; Shamma, 1986). The first stage in a spectro-temporal model is the auditory filter bank which performs the spectro-temporal equivalent of the spectral analysis that appears in the spectrogram. Figure 2 shows the output of a typical auditory filter bank when the input is the central portion of the [ae] in "past". As in Figure 1, the ordinate and abscissa are frequency and time, respectively, but in Figure 2 the time scale is greatly expanded. Whereas in Figure 1b, the vowel occupies about half of the figure width and contains over 40 pitch periods, in Figure 2, the vowel occupies the entire width of the figure and contains only four pitch periods. Each of the fine lines in Figure 2 shows the output of a single auditory filter as a plot of amplitude versus time. There are 189 channels in this filter bank and the surface that the filter outputs define is intended to represent the motion of the basilar membrane. The filter bank is described in greater detail in Part 1.A. The important point here is to observe the overall patterns of motion produced by vowels.

The set of three features that occur in the upper half of each cycle of the vowel are the second, third and fourth formants of [ae] as they appear within the pitch period. In

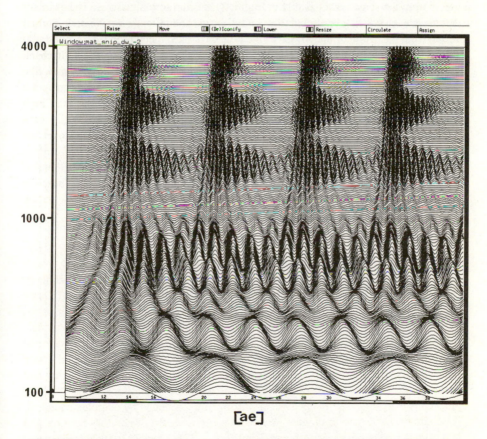

[ae]

FIG. 3.2   A cochleogram of four cycles of the [ae] in "past" produced by a gammatone auditory filterbank with 189 channels. The triangular objects are the formants. This representation shows that they have a distinctive shape that is not revealed in the spectrogram. The abscissa is time and the duration of each period is 8ms (f_0 = 125 Hz). The ordinate is filter centre-frequency on an ERB-rate scale.

two dimensions (frequency and time), the formants appear as triangular objects whose temporal extent decreases as formant number increases. When we include the third dimension (filter amplitude), the shape becomes that of a cone with its core parallel to the time axis. The interpretation of the first formant is more complex because, in that case, the temporal extent of the cone is greater than the pitch period and so the cones overlap and interact. Nevertheless, it is also, basically, a cone. Thus, from the auditory perspective, the basic pattern of a vowel is a set of four regularly recurring, temporally coordinated cones. This set of physical characteristics is probably sufficient to identify a stream of sounds as speech rather than some other pitch producing event like music.

The patterns of motion produced by four different vowels, [i], [ae], [a] and [u], are shown in Figure 3. All four vowels are from the same speaker and the [ae] in the second panel is from the same vowel as that in Figure 2. In order to maintain the same scale as Figure 2, each vowel is restricted to one pitch period and in each case the period was selected from the centre of the vowel. At the bottom of each panel in Figure 3, one can observe a single cycle of the fundamental of the vowel, and just above it, two cycles of the second harmonic. Both show the sinusoidal motion characteristic of resolved, or isolated, harmonics.

All of the formants of [ae] occupy separate regions of the spectrum and the first

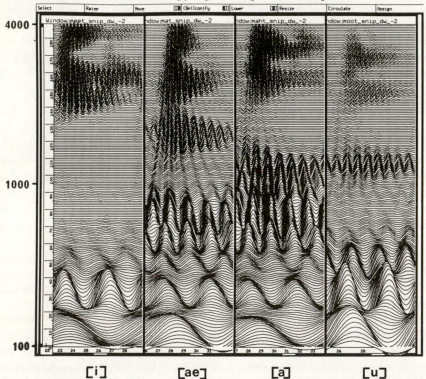

FIG. 3.3   Cochleograms of the four vowels [i], [ae], [a] and [u]. The position and strength of the formants identify the vowel.

formant is centred on the fourth and fifth harmonics. The first formant of [i] (leftmost panel) moves down from the position it occupied in [ae] into the region of the second harmonic, and the second formant moves up to encroach on the region of the third formant. The first formant of [a] (third panel) occupies the same region as it does in [ae] while the second formant moves down into the region adjacent to the first formant. Both the first and second formants of [u] move down relative to their positions in [ae]. In this case, however, the more striking change is the reduction in the amplitude of the second, third and fourth formants. Taken together these observations suggest that a general purpose speech machine would benefit from the inclusion of a feature extractor that, in one way or another, fitted a set of four cones to the pattern of motion in each pitch period, and then used the summary values concerning the positions and sizes of the cones to identify vowels. The temporal information in the taper of the cones should provide for much more accurate formant positioning and tracking than is possible from a simple spectral representation.

The temporal information also has other uses. For example, in the [a] (third panel), there is an extension to the end of the fourth formant which probably represents an irregularity in the speaker's glottal waveform. The same feature appears in the third and fourth formants of [i] and there is a hint of it in the fourth formant of both [ae] and [u]. Temporal features of this form could be useful in speaker identification or speaker authentication systems. Note that the feature would be integrated out in a purely spectral representation of speech. Other potential advantages of spectro-temporal models will be presented in Part 1. It is sufficient to note at this point that there is reason to believe that the extra temporal information in auditory models will enhance the capabilities of ASR machines when our models and computers expand to the point where we can cope with the higher data rates.

1. PERIPHERAL AUDITORY PROCESSING

In the cochlea, there are four rows of hair cells along the edge of the basilar membrane. The hair cells in conjunction with the primary auditory neurons convert the motion of the basilar membrane into a complex neural firing pattern that flows from the cochlea up the auditory nerve to the auditory cortex. There is now a reasonable degree of consensus concerning the major characteristics of the electro-mechanical operations performed by the cochlea, that is, the auditory filtering process and neural transduction process. We begin this part of the paper by describing a typical cochlea simulation that illustrates the important characteristics of, and recent advances in, cochlear processing.

The operations performed by the cochlea are often presented as if they were the only processing performed by the auditory system prior to speech recognition. In fact there are at least four operations, or groups of operations, that are applied to the neural firing pattern after it leaves the cochlea and before it reaches the speech recognition system, and each plays an important role in conditioning the signal. In the latter half of this section we outline three of the operations and attempt to put them in perspective with regard to cochlear processing. The remaining operation, localisation, is omitted for brevity.

A. Cochlear Processing

1. Auditory Filtering

The classic early work by von Bekesy (1960) suggested that the action of the basilar membrane was like that of a lowpass filter. In contrast, psychophysical experiments of the same era (Wegel & Lane, 1924) showed that, at moderate levels at least, the frequency selectivity of the human auditory system was better characterised by a bandpass filter function. The discrepancy between the basilar membrane data and the psychophysical data eventually led to the assumption that there must be a neural filtering mechanism in the auditory system beyond the cochlea, and that the performance of normal listeners was the result of a pair of cascaded filters, the first electro-mechanical, and the second neural (Houtgast, 1974).

Bekesy's experiments were performed on cadavers and the signals were presented at extremely high intensities. Over the past decade, advances in the Mossbauer technique have made it possible to measure the motion of the basilar membrane at ever lower intensities. As the results came in, it immediately became clear that, at all but the highest levels, the basilar membrane provides bandpass rather than lowpass filtering. The lowpass form presented by Bekesy was an artifact of the extreme signal levels required by the techniques available to him at the time.

The new data caused a revolution in our conception of the cochlea. It is now assumed that there is an active mechanism that sharpens the low-frequency skirt of the filter before neural transduction. Subsequent investigation has shown that there is surprisingly good agreement between the new physiological data and that summarised in psychophysical models of the human auditory filterbank (Schofield, 1985). Together these findings indicate that we can eliminate the neural sharpening stage in our models of the peripheral auditory system (de Boer, 1983), a simplification whose importance is difficult to overestimate. It would appear to indicate that the relatively simple auditory filterbanks used in most psychological models do provide a reasonable representation of cochlear filtering.

The Gammatone Filterbank: The operation of a typical filterbank is illustrated in Figure 4 with the aid of a pulse train with a repetition rate of 125 Hz shown in Figure 4a. The filterbank contains 94 channels with centre frequencies ranging from 100 to 4,000 Hz and there are four filters per critical band. Each line in panel (b) shows the output of one filter when the stimulus is the pulse train in panel (a). The general equation for the filter shape is given by the gammatone function which was originally used by physiologists (de Boer & de Jongh, 1978; Johannesma, 1972) to describe the filter responses they obtained in single unit studies with cats. The equation for the filter is:

$$gt(t) = t^{n-1} \exp(-2\pi bt) \cos(2\pi f_c t) \qquad (1)$$

where t is time, f_c is the filter centre frequency, n is the filter order and b is a bandwidth parameter. The term gammatone refers to the shape of the impulse response of the filter. The first two terms of the equation are the familiar gamma distribution from statistics and they define the envelope of the impulse response. The cosine term is a tone when the frequency is in the auditory range, and it provides the fine structure of the impulse response.

Patterson and Moore (1986) have reviewed the data on the shape of the human auditory filter and shown that the Roex filter shape suggested by Patterson, Nimmo-Smith, Weber and Milroy (1982) provides a good approximation to the human filter shape over a wide range of stimulus conditions. Recently, Schofield (1985) has shown that the gammatone function can provide a good fit to the human filter-shape data measured by Patterson (1976), indicating that the gammatone filter and the Roex filter are close relatives. The gammatone filter has the advantage of providing both a

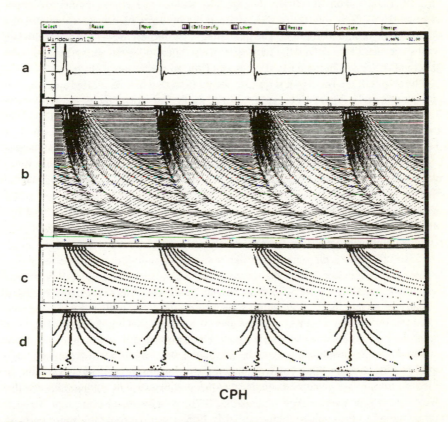

CPH

FIG. 3.4   The processing of a pulse train, or CPH wave, by the pulse ribbon model. The filterbank converts the wave (a) into a cochleogram (b) which the array of hair-cell simulators convert into a pulse ribbon, either without (c), or with (d), phase compensation.

spectral and a temporal representation of the filtering process. Accordingly a gammatone filterbank with parameter values that represent those found in human hearing has been developed, and it is this filterbank that underlies the illustrations in this part of the paper.

The gammatone expression was tuned to human hearing by (a) setting the filter order, n, to 4, (b) distributing the filters across frequency as suggested by Moore and Glasberg (1983), and (c) calculating the parameter b using the ERB function:

$$ERB(f_c) = 6.23 \times 10^{-6} f_c^2 + 93.39 \times 10^{-3} f_c + 28.52 \qquad (2)$$

and the scaling relationship

$$b = 1.019 \, ERB(f_c). \qquad (3)$$

Each filter is then convolved with the signal to produce one of the channels of output in panel (b) of Figure 4. The surface defined by the array of outputs represents the motion of the basilar membrane. The individual filter outputs are referred to as driving waves because they "drive" the hair cells in the sense of determining the temporal pattern of the spikes in the pulse streams that flow up the auditory nerve.

The output of the filterbank is quite different from that of a magnified spectrogram like that shown in Figure 1b because the bandwidth of the filter increases with centre frequency in the auditory filterbank. The driving waves in the lower part of Figure 4b are from relatively narrow filters centred in the region of the first four harmonics of the pulse train, and they are essentially sinusoidal in shape. Those in the middle part of the panel are from wider filters centred near harmonics 5 to 12, and they are more like amplitude-modulated sinusoids. The "carrier" frequency is approximately the centre frequency of the filter and the "modulation" frequency is the repetition rate of the pulse train. The modulation depth increases with centre frequency as the filter broadens and the attenuation of adjacent harmonics decreases. The driving waves in the upper part of panel (b) are from relatively wide filters centred near harmonics 13 to 32. In this region, the outputs are like a stream of individual impulse responses because the integration time of the filter is short with respect to the repetition rate of the pulse train. In a system with proportional bandwidth, the pattern of membrane motion is relatively independent of the repetition rate of the stimulus; the cycles move closer together as the pitch rises and the energy associated with individual harmonics moves up the figure somewhat, but the pattern remains largely unchanged.

The pronounced rightwards skew in the lower half of the filterbank output is also caused by the fact that filter bandwidth increases with centre frequency. But there is evidence from phase perception studies that the auditory system compensates for the phase lag that produces the skew (Patterson, 1987b). As a result, we often apply a phase compensation to the cochleogram in order to bring together vertically those parts of the pattern that belong to one pitch period of the original sound. The vowel cochleograms presented in the Introduction are a case in point. They were generated by a gammatone filterbank and phase-compensated to align the formants.

2. Neural Transduction

The motion of the basilar membrane is converted into nerve impulses by the hair cells and the primary auditory neurones of the eighth nerve. Physiological research over the past two decades has revealed several important facts about neural transduction:

1) The hair cell applies something like logarithmic compression to the amplitude of the driving wave.
2) The adaptation we observe in the auditory nerve takes place in the hair cell and the synaptic cleft that separates it from the primary neurone that it drives.
3) There are few cross connections in this part of the system; by and large, the outer hair cells amplify membrane motion for the inner hair cell, which in turn drives the primary neurone.

These advances have led the physiologists to suggest relatively simple, "reservoir" models of neural transduction (Schwid and Geisler, 1982; Meddis, 1986). In practical terms, it would appear that a reasonable approximation is provided by a device consisting of a logarithmic compressor followed by a peak picker that has one fast and one slow adaptation parameter. Such a unit produces a phase-locked stream of pulses that preserves information concerning the times between the positive peaks in the wave, like the streams observed in auditory nerve fibers.

The Initial Pulse Ribbon: The cochlea simulation uses the hair-cell simulation suggested by Meddis (1986). A bank of "hair cells" converts the 96 driving waves into 96 pulse streams as illustrated in Fig. 4c. Each pulse stream is intended to represent the output of all the fibers associated with one frequency channel. In short, the stochastic properties of neural transduction are ignored for the moment, and a volley mechanism of some sort is assumed. In this case, sinusoidal driving waves like those in the lower portion of panel (b) are converted into regular pulse streams with one pulse per cycle as shown at the bottom of panel (c). Modulated driving waves like those at the top of panel (b) are converted into modulated pulse streams in which bursts of pulses are regularly separated by gaps as shown at the top of panel (c). The period of the carrier frequency is equal to the time between pulses within a burst and the period of the modulation frequency is equal to the time between corresponding pulses in successive bursts.

Collectively, the array of pulse streams is referred to as the "initial pulse ribbon" and it provides an overview of the information flowing up the auditory system from the cochlea. The horizontal dimension of the ribbon is "time since the sound reached the eardrum"; the vertical dimension is "auditory-filter centre frequency" which is a roughly logarithmic frequency scale. If the brightness of each channel were varied to reflect its current amplitude, the initial pulse ribbon would be like a spectrogram with an expanded time scale. For a periodic sound, the pattern repeats on the ribbon and the rate of repetition corresponds to the pitch of the sound. $1 timbreTimbre corresponds to the pattern of pulses within the cycle. The pattern has a spectral dimension (vertical) as in traditional spectral models, but it also has a temporal dimension (horizontal), and the fine-grain information on the latter dimension enables the ribbon to represent phase-related timbre changes.

The initial pulse ribbon, then, is a device for presenting the temporal information and the phase information of the auditory nerve, in a form where we can better appreciate the patterns of information generated by complex sounds like music and speech. It is not intended to be new or controversial but rather to provide a simplified view of what comes out of the cochlea to support further research.

The bottom panel of Figure 4 shows the initial pulse ribbon produced by the pulse train when phase compensation is included in the operations. The compensation brings together in a vertical column those pulses associated with the largest peaks in the cochleogram, and it helps to emphasise the natural symmetry of this stimulus. For comparison, the phase-compensated pulse ribbon produced by the [ae] of Figure 2 is presented in Figure 5. The largest cochleogram peaks are also aligned in this figure, but the formants impose a spectro-temporal weighting that imparts a strong left/right

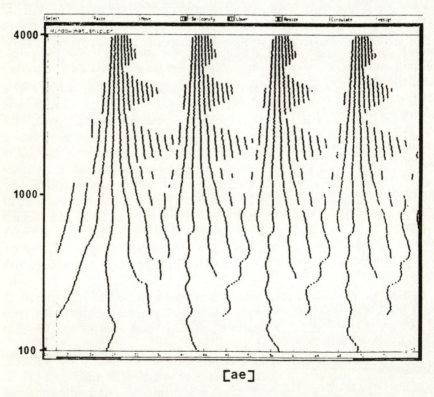

[ae]

FIG. 3.5   The initial pulse ribbon produced by four cycles of the [ae] in "past". Note that this reduced representation preserves the basic pattern of information in the cochleogram of Figure 2.

asymmetry, an asymmetry which is characteristic of voiced speech sounds. Note also that the pulse ribbon preserves the basic information of the corresponding cochleogram even though it requires less than one tenth the bandwidth.

B. Neural Peripheral Processing

There are now a number of physiological and psychological models of hearing that include some representation of auditory neural processing as well as cochlear processing. It is still the case, however, that physiological models tend to emphasize cochlear processing and include only the earliest stages of the neural processing. As a result, they are usually less appropriate as preprocessors for ASR than psychological models which combine functional models of cochlear processing with functional models of more central processes, such as pitch perception. There is not space in a chapter this size to compare physiological and psychological models of hearing with regard to their suitability as ASR preprocessors. Rather we will present one psychological model which makes an explicit attempt to be comprehensive and to balance the level of complexity used in the representations of cochlear and neural processing.

The "pulse ribbon" model of hearing (Patterson, 1987a) was originally created to provide a bridge between the output of the cochlea as observed in single nerve fibres of small mammals stimulated by simple sounds, and the sensations that humans hear when stimulated by complex sounds like music and speech. The model has five stages: the first two stages simulate auditory filtering and neural transduction and they form the cochlea simulation just described in Section A. With regard to cochlear processing, the pulse ribbon model is like most other psychological models, attempting to summarise our knowledge concerning frequency selectivity and neural transduction in the form of an array of pulse streams.

The remaining three stages transform this initial pulse ribbon using operations that are intended to characterise phase perception, pitch perception and timbre perception, respectively. Together they illustrate the kind of neural processing required to convert the output of the cochlea into stabilised patterns that represent the perceptions, or auditory images, produced by sounds. In the model these stabilised pulse patterns are the output of the peripheral auditory system and the input to more central systems like those for speech and music.

1. Phase Perception

In 1947 Mathes and Miller proved that, contrary to previous suggestions (Helmholtz, 1875, 1912), the auditory system is not phase deaf. They showed that changes in the envelopes of high-frequency driving waves change the timbre of the sound. Confirmations and extentions of their findings have been reported at regular intervals since that time (for a review see Patterson, 1987b). For over 50 years, then, throughout the development of spectral front-ends for speech processing, we have known that strictly spectral models of auditory processing must ultimately fail, and that, at best, these models are a practical simplification of peripheral processing.

With hindsight, there are two obvious reasons for ignoring the data on phase sensitivity, over and above the fact that they would have rendered models unacceptably complex at that time: firstly, the timbre changes produced by phase changes were not thought important for speech perception and secondly, there were no coherent models of phase perception to unify the observations and suggest how it might be implemented. Recent research, however, has changed both of these positions. With regard to the first, it is now clear that phase changes produce relatively strong perceptual effects (Carlson et al, 1980), and that they almost undoubtedly do play a role in vowel discrimination (Tranmuller, 1988). Furthermore, there is the hint that it is the proper handling of phase information that enables the auditory system to perform so much better than speech recognisers in reverberant environments. With regard to the second, coherent models of phase perception are beginning to appear (Patterson, 1987b; Wakefield, 1987).

This subsection describes a series of phase experiments to illustrate the advances that have been made in our understanding. The experiments are from Patterson (1987b) and they were performed to determine our sensitivity to changes in the envelopes of the driving waves, changes introduced by local alterations of the phase spectrum. In each case, the stimuli were composed of 31 equal-amplitude harmonics of a fundamental, fo, and all that varied was the phase spectrum of the stimulus. The stimuli were "alternating-phase" waves in which all of the odd harmonics were in cosine phase while all of the even harmonics were in some other fixed phase, D. Figure 6a shows the alternating-phase wave when D is 40 degrees. When D is 0 the wave is a pulse train, or cosine-phase wave. As D increases the secondary peak in the middle of the cycle grows and eventually we hear a timbre change. In the mid- to high-frequency channels of the filterbank, the secondary peak in the sound wave causes a local maximum in the envelope of the driving wave midway between the main envelope peaks (panel b) and the size of the local maximum increases with D. When D is large, the local maxima cause the pulse stream generators to produce an extra column of pulses in the initial pulse ribbon (compare Figures 4c and 6c) and it is these pulses that are assumed to produce the timbre change. The alternating-phase stimulus was used to map out the existence region for local phase changes.

The wave in Fig. 6a is just discriminable from a cosine-phase wave when the fundamental is 125 Hz and the level is 45 dB/component. When f_0 is lowered by an octave, the period of the wave doubles. In this case, the pulse generators have effectively twice as many pulses to assign to each cycle of the driving wave and the local maxima appear in the pulse ribbon at a lower D value. Thus, the model predicts that timbre threshold will be strongly affected by the pitch of the stimulus, and this is indeed the case. The firing rates of auditory nerve fibers increase with stimulus level which suggests that the sustained firing rates of the pulse generators in the model should vary with stimulus level. Increasing the model rates causes the local maxima in the driving waves to appear in the pulse ribbon at a lower D value and so the model predicts that timbre threshold will vary inversely with stimulus level, and this prediction is also borne out by the data. Thus, it would appear that a pulse ribbon model can account for the timbre changes associated with envelope changes in terms of the firing rates of the

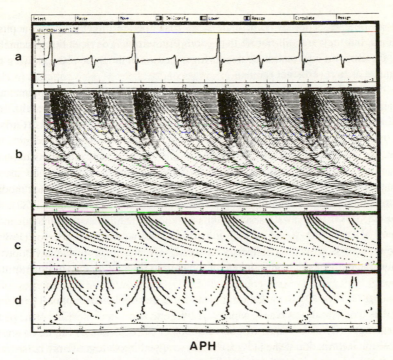

APH

FIG. 3.6   The processing of an APH wave by the pulse ribbon model (D = 40 degrees). The filterbank converts the wave (a) into a cochleogram (b) which the array of hair-cell simulators convert into a pulse ribbon, either without (c), or with (d), phase compensation. Note that the secondary pulse in the waveform produces a secondary ridge in each cycle of the cochleogram. The resulting feature in the pulse ribbon is assumed to be the cue that mediates the timbre change associated with this stimulus.

pulse stream generators, and conversely, the data from alternating-phase experiments can be used to set the parameter values in the model.

2. Pitch Extraction

The purpose of the fourth stage of the model is to determine the pitch of the sound. Originally, speech recognition devices extracted the pitch value from a lowpass filtered version of the acoustic waveform. Although this works reasonably well when the speech occurs in a quiet environment, it fails when the speech occurs in a noisy environment. More recently, speech and hearing models have come to use pitch extractors based on one of the "central spectrum" models of pitch perception (Wightman, 1973; Goldstein 1973; Terhardt, 1974). In their original forms, these models ignored the timing information in the driving waves and estimated the pitch solely on the basis of the power, or overall firing rate, in each channel. In essence, it was argued that the overall-rate information was sufficient to explain the psychophysical data so long as optimal use was made of that information. These pitch extractors operate better in noise than those that operate directly on the acoustic waveform, but they are still not all that good. Furthermore, devices that discard the fine-grain temporal information do not perform well when the peak of the glottal pulse is degraded as in reverberant rooms.

For these and several other reasons, a number of groups have chosen to investigate the potential of spectro-temporal models which, as the name suggests, use the temporal, as well as the spectral, information (Young and Sachs, 1979; Goldstein and Srulovicz, 1977; Lyon, 1984; Gardner and Uppal, 1986; Cooke, 1986; Beet, Moore and Tomlinson, 1986; Patterson, 1987a). At the output of the cochlea, a periodic sound produces a repeating pulse pattern (Figures 4d and 6d) and the repetition rate of the pattern provides a good estimate of the pitch of the sound. The voiced parts of speech are quasi-periodic sounds and they also produce repeating pulse ribbons as illustrated in Figure 5. Spectro-temporal models make use of the spectral information in the sense that they separate the signal energy into different frequency bands. In addition, however, there is a second frequency analysis, -- a temporal analysis, performed neurally, that extracts the repetition rate of the pattern flowing up the auditory system.

The Spiral Processor: One attempt to solve the problem of temporal frequency analysis is the "spiral processor" suggested by Patterson (1986, 1987a). Briefly, the temporal regularity observed in the pulse ribbons of periodic sounds can be converted into position information if the pulse ribbon is wrapped into a logarithmic spiral, base two. For example, consider the pulse ribbon associated with the alternative-phasing wave (Figure 6d). If we assume that the temporal window on which the periodicity mechanism operates is 72 ms in duration, then it will contain 9 cycles of the pulse ribbon at any one moment as shown in the upper panel of Figure 7. If this pulse ribbon is wrapped into a spiral, base 2, the result is the 9-cycle spiral ribbon shown in Figure 7b. The threads of the pulse ribbon in panel (a) become a set of concentric spirals in panel (b). The outer and inner strands of the spiral ribbon contain the pulse streams from the 1st and 96th channels, respectively.

The pulses appear at the centre of the spiral as they are generated and flow along the spiral as time progresses, dropping off at the outer end 72 ms after appearing. So time itself keeps track of the pulses as they are being correlated with their neighbours in time and space. The stimulus occupies four revolutions of the spiral, and at the moment shown, four of the vertical columns that mark cycles on the pulse ribbon are themselves lined up on one spoke of the spiral, the vertical spoke emanating from the centre of the spiral. A unit monitoring this spoke would note above average activity at this instant and so serve as a detector for 125 Hz. A stable display of the current pitch pattern can be obtained from the continuously flowing spiral ribbon, by strobing the display when the pulse coincidence occurs. The angles between the spokes are the same no matter what the note; it is only the orientation of the spoke pattern that changes when the pitch is altered. As the pitch rises, the spokes rotate clockwise as a unit and the pattern completes one full revolution as the pitch rises an octave. Computationally, the spiral processor is just a mapping that warps the space through which the pulses

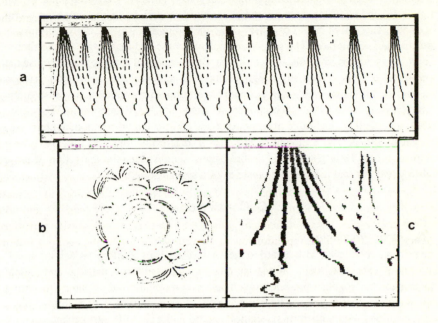

FIG. 3.7   Pitch extraction and timbre stabilisation in the pulse ribbon model. The phase compensated pulse ribbon (a) is wrapped into a logarithmic spiral (b) to extract the pitch, and wrapped into a cylindrical pulse ribbon (c), with circumference equal to the pitch period, to stabilise the repeating pulse pattern.

flow, so that clusters of pulses that repeat in time come together in space for an instant and produce a secondary pulse indicating the pitch of the sound. Since it is a mapping it can be implemented as a table look-up operation, which makes it a relatively efficient process.

3. Timbre Stabilisation

The pulse patterns produced by successive cycles of a periodic wave are highly correlated. The timbre of the sound is coded in these pulse patterns and so one should combine them to obtain the best estimate of timbre in the statistical sense. In the pulse ribbon model this is accomplished, once the pitch of the source is known, by wrapping the pulse ribbon around a cylinder whose circumference is the period of the original sound. In this case, successive cycles of the ribbon fall on top of each other and form a stabilised image of the timbre pattern for as long as the sound is stationary. When the input is noise, the pulse streams are not periodic and the timbre pattern is a rectangular random dot pattern no matter what the diameter of the cylinder.

The timbre pattern for the alternating-phase wave is shown in panel (c). For convenience, a planar display is used as if the cylindrical ribbon had been slit down the back and flattened out. There are approximately 4000 pulses in the initial pulse ribbon of panel (a) and all of them are plotted in panel (c) as well. However, since the sound is periodic, successive cycles of pulses coincide and in this way the correlated timbre information is combined. The column of pulses on the righthand side of the timbre pattern gives the sound its distinctive timbre. Purely spectral models that only use the overall-rate of firing effectively integrate across the temporal dimension of the ribbon and obscure this feature. Although the pitch of complex sounds is singularly insensitive to the phase of their constituent components (Patterson, 1973; Patterson and Wightman, 1976), nevertheless, the timbre of complex sounds is affected by component phase (see Patterson, 1987b, for a review), and vowel discriminations are largely timbre discriminations. Thus, a stabilised timbre pattern should assist the extraction of those auditory features that indicate the presence of a speech sound.

C. Conclusion

1. Cochlear Processing

The primary conclusion with regard to the earliest stages of auditory processing is that there now exist relatively simple simulations of auditory filtering and neural transduction that together provide a much better representation of cochlear processing than does the spectrogram. The replacement of spectrographic and similar place representations with a cochlea simulation should enhance ASR performance even if the remaining stages of auditory processing are ignored.

2. Neural Processing

Phase: The auditory system is phase-sensitive and the inclusion of a competent neural phase mechanism should improve ASR performance in the areas of speaker identification and resistance to reverberation.

Pitch: Until recently, pitch was not thought to be a particularly important variable in speech recognition. It was argued that although pitch is a major determinant of prosody, nevertheless, large changes in prosody do not prevent one recognising individual words in a phrase or sentence. The pulse ribbon model leads us to conclude that pitch is not just one of many speech features, it is the key feature that makes it possible to stabilise the timbre of the voiced parts of speech and so extract the remaining speech features more effectively. A similar concept already exists in speech research, where the use of pitch information to create a better vowel representation is referred to as "pitch-synchronous feature extraction" (Seneff, 1984). However, the technique is based on driving-wave envelopes rather than neural firing patterns, and this will probably lead to a timbre image that is not quite as well focused.

In speech, the pitch varies in the short term over a range of about an octave. But much of the time, the rate of change is relatively slow when measured in auditory terms. In this case, the pitch extractor, whatever its form, can track the pitch and feed the current value forward so that the timbre pattern can be continuously adjusted to maintain a stable image. The image will rise or fall a little on the timbre display but the variation will be small relative to the change in pitch, and the pattern will remain identifiable.

Timbre: It is now possible to create a stabilised auditory image of stationary sounds, and the concentration of timbre information on the cylindrical pulse ribbon should assist feature extraction and speech segmentation. Currently auditory front-ends send a frame of timbre information forward to the next module in the speech processor every n milliseconds, even if there is no sound coming in. If, instead, the auditory front-end were set to check whether the pattern had changed, and to send a frame forward only when there was a significant change in the pattern, it would greatly reduce the computational load on the recognition system.

2. RECOGNITION

A. Background

In Part 2 we switch our attention to psycholinguistic work on the understanding of spoken language. Of course this differs from psychoacoustic research primarily in the level of processing under consideration. But the flavour of the research is also very different. Whereas psychoacousticians know, for instance, the nature of the operations performed on auditory signals by the basilar membrane and the hair-cell array, and tie their theorising closely to the physical characteristics of these structures, psycholinguists can call on no such physical constraints. Psycholinguists are cognitive psychologists, and their conceptual repertoire is accordingly restricted to cognitive constructs. The most central of these in the present context is recognition, i.e. acknowledgement that an input has been previously encountered. Obviously the concept of storage in memory is central to recognition, and so is the notion of a representation, or code in terms of which an input and a stored form can be matched with one another so that recognition can be achieved. In the following sections we discuss the basic characteristics of the recognition task as seen by psycholinguists, and the assumptions which underlie psycholinguistic research on the processing of spoken language. As we stated above, we examine this processing only as far as the point at which spoken word recognition has been accomplished. Although there is a substantial body of psycholinguistic research on higher levels of processing, we will omit it entirely, for several reasons: it would extend the present discussion out of proportion to the rest of this chapter; it is discussed elsewhere in this book; and it makes no separate contribution to the problem of interfacing psychoacoustic work on auditory perception with psycholinguistic work on speech recognition.

B. Nature of the Recognition Task

Recognition involves matching an input to a pre-stored representation. In the case of speech recognition the input is an auditory representation and the pre-stored representation is conceptual; so speech recognition consists in the translation of sound to meaning. The goal of the task is achieving an internal representation in the recogniser that is equivalent to an internal representation in a communicator-recognition of the communicator's "message". The cognitive system takes as input a representation which is the output of auditory preprocessing, and it outputs in turn a selection from its stored set of sound-meaning associates.

Precisely how it does this is in part determined by the characteristics of these stored meaning representations themselves. The set of potential messages is infinite. But recognisers do not have infinite storage capacity. Therefore the stored set of representations, which is usually termed the *lexicon*, cannot possibly include every message a recogniser might potentially encounter. The set of representations in the lexicon must be *finite*, and it must consist of *discrete* units.

Part of the process of translating sound into meaning, therefore, must consist in determining which parts of a signal correspond to which discrete stored units. This is essentially a *segmentation* problem. Logically, the only segmentation of a speech signal which is required is segmentation into lexical units; as we shall see below, however, other segmentation units may be warranted in practice.

C. The Lexicon

Several characteristics of the lexical store are relevant to consideration of the segmentation issue. Firstly, the size of the discrete units represented in the lexicon must be highly variable. It is reasonable to suppose that many orthographically defined words will merit a separate stored representation, though of course there is no reason to suggest that it is a necessary criterion that each lexical representation be a separate orthographic word. Nor is it by itself a sufficient criterion, since orthographic words exist which have no separate conceptual representation (e.g. *kith*, which occurs now only in *kith and kin*); grammatical words (*to*, *the*, *but* etc.), whose "meaning" is their function in context, similarly present difficulties of conceptual definition. Some studies of the mental lexicon (e.g. Friederici & Schoenle, 1980) have proposed that grammatical words are represented separately and differently from the greater part of the lexical stock. Similarly, it has been suggested (e.g. by Taft, 1988) that affixal or stem morphemes may be stored as separate units (in English, for example, this would mean such separate entries as *un-*, *re-*, *-mit*, *-vert*, *-ment*, *-ish* etc.; but in highly affixing languages such as Turkish the set of potential stored morphemes would be very large indeed). It has also been proposed that certain stored units may contain sequences of words, forming, for instance, idioms such as *kick the bucket* (Swinney & Cutler, 1979) or highly frequent expressions such as *good morning* (van Lancker, 1975). Since even monomorphemic words can vary dramatically in length (*owe*, *salmagundi*), it is clear that the stored representations in the lexicon will be highly heterogeneous. Aitchison (1987) reviews recent research on the structure of the mental lexicon.

Secondly, whatever the constitution of the stored set of representations, its size is sure to be very large. Estimates of the educated adult language user's vocabulary have proposed an average size of 150,000 words (Seashore & Eckerson, 1940). To search a set of this size at a thousand items per second would take several minutes. Yet this is hardly a realistic estimate of lexical access time for a human recogniser (nor is it an acceptable goal for a commercial automatic recogniser). Both the size and the heterogeneity of the lexicon have implications for prelexical aspects of the recognition process, as will be outlined below.

D. The Normalisation Issue

The speech signal corresponding to a particular lexical representation is not a fixed acoustic form. It is no exaggeration to say that even two productions of the same utterance by the same speaker speaking on the same occasion at the same rate will not be completely identical. But within-speaker variability is tiny compared to the enormous variability across speakers and across occasions. Speakers differ widely in the length and shape of their vocal tracts, as a function of age, sex and other physical characteristics; productions of a given sound by a large adult male and by a small child have little in common. Situation-specific variations include the speaker's current physiological state; the voice can change when the speaker is tired, for instance, or as a result of temporary changes in vocal tract shape such as a swollen or anaesthetised mouth, a pipe clenched between the teeth, or a mouthful of food. Other situational variables include distance between speaker and hearer, intervening barriers, and background noise. Yet acoustic signals which (for all these reasons) are very widely varying indeed are nevertheless perceived by listeners as the same speech event. For this to happen, there has to be some way of factoring out the speaker- and situation-specific contributions. This is called the problem of *normalisation* across speakers.

A further source of variability is due to different varieties, or dialects, of a given language. Sounds can be articulated very differently in different dialects (compare, for instance, English /r/ as spoken in Kansas and in Boston, in Bombay, Aberdeen, Sydney, Somerset and Surrey). dialects also differ in the size of their phonemic repertoire (Southern British English uses different vowels in each of *book, but* and *boot,* but Scottish English has the same vowel in *book* and *boot,* and a different vowel in *but,* while Northern British English has the same vowel in *book* and *but* but a different vowel in *boot.*) Thus listeners have to normalise for dialect variability as well. At the word level, variability also arises due to speech style, or register, and (often related to this) speech rate. Consider the two words "did you". In formal speech they would be pronounced [dIdju]; a phonetic transcription shows five separate segments. A more casual style allows for the [d] and [j] to palatalise to an affricate [dZ], giving [dIdZu]. If the two words occur at the beginning of a phrase, the entire first syllable will often be dropped, leaving only the affrication as a trace of the word "did": "[dZu] see that?" Finally, in appropriate contexts the vowel of "you" can be reduced or lost entirely: "[dZ@] see it?"; "[dZit] yet?" In that latter phrase the single affricate [dZ] is performing the function of [dIdju] in a formal, precise utterance of "did you eat yet?"; but there is no segmental overlap between the two transcriptions.

At the phoneme level, variability is further complicated by the phenomenon of coarticulation. Phonetic segments may be spoken quite differently as a function of the other segments which surround them in a particular utterance. Stop consonants are particularly sensitive to the identity of the following vowel; thus spectrograms of the words "past" and "pieced" look quite different in the initial consonant as well as in the vowel portions. In some cases these differences can even be noticed by the speaker (/k/ is articulated further forward in the vocal tract in speaking "keen" than in speaking "corn"). Moreover, coarticulation effects are not confined to immediately adjacent segments; their influence can stretch both forwards and backwards over several segments. Consider the utterance "she has to spruce herself up"; in most cases, the lip-rounding for the [u] in "spruce" is fully in place by the utterance of the word-initial [s], or even during the preceding syllable; and it does not disappear until well into the word "herself".

This extreme variability means, simply, that if the lexicon were to store an exact acoustic representation for every possible form in which a given lexical unit might be presented as a speech signal, it would need infinite storage capacity. Therefore the lexical representation of the input signal, i.e. the sound component of the sound-meaning pairing, must be in a relatively *abstract* (or normalised) form. In consequence, the progression from auditory featuresto the input representation for lexical access necessarily involves a process of *transformation*.

E. The Continuity Issue

Units of lexical representation (words) are all that it is necessary to locate in the input. But the nature of auditory linguistic input is that it extends over time - a portion of input corresponding to a particular lexical form is not simultaneously available in its entirety. Moreover, only rarely are recognisers presented with isolated lexical items. Most speech signals are made up of a stream of words, and the stream is effectively continuous in that momentary discontinuities within it do not correspond systematically to its linguistic structure.

The importance of the continuity issue for speech recognition has been neglected, simply because the majority of psycholinguistic studies of lexical storage and retrieval have been carried out in the visual domain. In nearly all orthographies, representations of linguistic messages in the visual domain consist of discontinuous units: words, which are made up in turn (depending on the orthography) of letters, syllables or the like. Under such circumstances, segmentation is no problem. Whatever the orthography, explicit markers in the input (i.e. spaces) signify the boundaries of portions of the input corresponding to lexical units; each of these units may then be further subdivided into elements which offer a possible subclassification scheme for the lexicon and hence a possible route for efficient lexical access. segmentation in the auditory domain would be similarly unproblematic if explicit boundary markers signalled which parts of the signal belonged together in a single lexical unit. Years of research in speech science, however, have failed to isolate reliable cues to lexical boundaries. One way round this problem is simply to match arbitrary portions of the auditory input (subject, of course, to suitable transformation) against lexical templates. This crude process, in a number of different guises, is in fact the basis of all automatic speech recognition systems currently in commercial production. Such template-matching procedures are, however, extremely inefficient. Firstly, they involve a large number of futile access attempts, since the heterogeneity of lexical units means that the duration of the string to be tested cannot be predicted. Secondly, since they invoke a simple search procedure, the large size of the lexical stock means that each attempt at access requires a long search. This is one reason why all current commercial automatic speech recognisers are limited to very small vocabularies.

The problem of *segmentation* under conditions of *continuity* suggests that prelexical classification of speech signals into some sub-word-level representation might enable a more efficient system of lexical access. As letters or syllables in orthography open up the possibility of classification within the lexicon and an access procedure based on this classification, so do sublexical units in the auditory domain. This overcomes the necessity for simple search procedures in lexical access, and hence removes the problem of the impracticable amount of time required to search a vocabulary of the size used by human recognisers. But the greatest advantage of a sublexical representation is that the set of potential units would be very much smaller than the set of units in the lexicon. However large and heterogeneous the lexical stock, any lexical item could be decomposed into a selection from a small and finite set of sublexical units. The normalisation issue and the consequent necessity of *transformation* provides another argument in favour of an intermediate level of representation between auditory featuresand lexical input. If transformation is necessary in any case, then transformation into a small set of possibilities will be far easier than transformation into a large set of possibilities.

F. Prelexical Representations

Psycholinguists have devoted a great deal of research effort to investigating the form that prelexical representations should take. For a segment of a speech signal to function as such a unit of representation, there are three conditions which it should meet:

1. The segments themselves, at whatever level they are, must be reasonably distinguishable in the speech signal. Note that this does not imply that they must have explicitly marked boundaries. If the boundaries of any sublexical unit were explicitly marked, then the boundaries of words would *ipso facto* be explicitly marked, but, as we have already observed, this is not the case.

2. The whole utterance must be characterisable as a string of the segments in question, with no parts of the utterance unaccounted for. (Thus although fricative noise might satisfy the first requirement, it is not acceptable to propose the interval from one fricative to the next as a potential sublexical unit of representation, since utterances may contain no fricatives at all.)

3. The units must correspond in some reliable way to lexical units. That is, if the unit in question is not necessarily sublexical, then some simple and predictable translation from the prelexical unit to the lexical unit should be possible.

Most current models of lexical storage and retrieval for spoken word recognition assume that (for the theoretical reasons outlined above) human recognition does involve some prelexical level of representation. It is assumed that this representation encodes the input in a form which can serve to access the lexicon efficiently, i.e. it corresponds to the code used on the "sound" side of the lexical sound-meaning pairings. In practice, the most obvious candidates for the role of intermediate representation have been the units of analysis used by linguistic science. The phoneme has been the most popular choice because (by definition) it is the smallest linguistic unit into which speech can be sequentially decomposed. The syllable is the second most popular choice; it is the smallest linguistic unit which can be independently uttered (with the exception, admittedly, of those phonemes which are realised as hisses or buzzes).

A great deal is known about the nature and manner of use of acoustic cues for identifying and distinguishing between phonemes, from speech perception work within linguistics and phonetics; see Pisoni and Luce (1986) and Jusczyk (1986) for reviews of this work. The most central issue in this debate for decades has been the question of invariance (see Perkell & Klatt 1986), i.e. the degree to which acoustic cues to phonemes can be said to possess invariant properties which are necessarily present whenever the phoneme is uttered, and which are therefore resistant to the sources of variation described in section D above. Insofar as syllables are made up of phonemes, this work is equally relevant to the perception and identification of syllables.

But this body of research, which has been conducted principally by phoneticians, is to a certain extent orthogonal to the psychological question of whether either phonemes or syllables are a necessary or appropriate level of representation for lexical access from auditory input. The question at issue here is, chiefly, whether phonemes or syllables constitute the kind of representation which could be output from auditory preprocessing, or, if not, whether the auditory features output by the preprocessor could readily be translated into either phonemes or syllables. The debate within psycholinguistics continues, and the evidence is mixed. On the one hand, there is by now a fairly substantial body of evidence that the syllable is a natural segmentation unit, at least for French (see Mehler, 1981, or Segui, 1984, for a review of this evidence). But syllabic segmentation effects which have been demonstrated in the recognition of French do not appear in the recognition of English (Cutler, Mehler, Norris & Segui, 1986; Norris & Cutler, 1988). For English, Pisoni (1981; see also Pisoni, Nusbaum, Luce & Slowiaczek, 1985) has argued that phonemes are the most useful segmentation units.

Other units have been proposed by speech engineers and psychologists in recent years; these include units both above the phonemic level (e.g. demisyllables: Fujimura & Lovins, 1978, 1982; diphones: Klatt, 1979) and below it, (e.g featural representations: McClelland & Elman, 1986; spectral templates: Klatt, 1979). It is generally the case that models of auditory word recognition which have assumed a level of representation in terms of a linguistic unit such as the phonological feature (McClelland & Elman, 1986), the phoneme (Marslen-Wilson, 1980; McClelland & Elman, 1986) or the syllable (Mehler, 1981; Segui, 1984) have arisen from within cognitive psychology, and have not been directly concerned with questions of recogniser implementation. Non-linguistic units such as diphones (Klatt, 1979) or demisyllables (Fujimura & Lovins, 1978, 1982) have largely been proposed by researchers who are concerned more with implementation than with psychological modelling.

G. The Universality Issue

In the above discussion a simplifying assumption has been adopted, namely that the three levels of representation considered, auditory representations output by the preprocessor, input representations to the lexicon, and intermediate representations if any, will be the same for all speech perception operations. This is not necessarily the case. Precisely in the area covered above there exists considerable variation across languages. For example, there is variation in what may potentially constitute a lexical unit, whereby relatively uninflected languages such as Chinese contrast with highly inflected languages such as Turkish. Similarly, there is variation in the potential characteristics of lexical input representations. Here there is a major distinction in the domain of prosody, between languages which use prosody to distinguish between lexical units and languages which do not. The former group includes tone languages such as Chinese and Thai, and lexical stress languages such as English and Russian. The latter group (which is larger) includes fixed stress languages such as Polish or Hungarian, and all non-tone non-stress languages such as French. Finally, there is considerable variation across languages in the variety and characteristics of the linguistic units which are presented as viable candidates for prelexical representation. The number of vowels in a language can vary from as few as three to as many as twelve (English has more than twice as many vowels as Japanese, for example). Syllable structure can vary from languages which allow only or almost only consonant -+ -vowel syllables (Japanese is one of the latter, for instance) to languages like English, in which syllables may be as different in structure as *a* and *strange*, and in which stress patterns result in a wide discrepancy in acoustic-phonetic clarity between the realisation of stressed and unstressed syllables. Syllable boundaries, likewise, may be phonologically distinct (as they are in languages with regular syllable structure, for instance Japanese) or indistinct (as they are at the on set of many unstressed syllables in stress languages like English).

These sources of variation allow for the possibility that the very nature of the linguistic material to be processed may affect the way it is processed. Psycholinguistic models of word recognition have paid little attention to this possibility. Again, it is perhaps the bias of lexical modelling towards the visual domain which has obscured relevant cross-linguistic variation (though recently psycholinguists working in the visual domain have begun to examine the possibility that the nature of an orthographic code can affect the nature of the reading process - see Henderson, 1984).

There is a sense in which the interests of the cognitive psychologist here parallel, in a fortuitous but potentially productive way, the interests of the designer of a practical speech recogniser. The cognitive psychologist is concerned with the nature of the human recognition system, rather than the nature of the recognition system for any particular language. The striking characteristic of the human language acquisition system is that it acquires any natural human language with equal success; the mental capability of a newborn child, irrespective of its parentage, is not biased towards acquisition of one language rather than another. Thus if there prove to be language-specific variations in such aspects of speech recognition as the nature of prelexical representations, the cognitive psychologist is concerned to distinguish what is necessary to the recognition system from what is possible, i.e. to distinguish what is universal to the recognition process in all language users from what is specific to processing by users of a particular language. Universal features will be obligatory components of a model of human language processing; language-specific variations will comprise a repertoire of optional components from which the processor will select those components which best cope with the nature of the input.

In a similar way, the designer of a recogniser may employ knowledge of universal versus language-specific characteristics of the human recognition process to constrain the architecture of a system, by focussing on the design of those components which are universal to all human language processors.

Cross-linguistic study of auditory recognition within psycholinguistics is in its infancy (Cutler, 1985). Very recently, however, evidence has been found for a cross-linguistic difference in speech segmentation strategies, which may in turn imply a corresponding difference in the nature of prelexical or lexical input representations; Cutler, Mehler, Norris and Segui (1986) have produced evidence that the syllable is an effective segmentation unit for French but not for English. This suggests that psycholinguists may indeed need to develop a larger language-universal framework within which such results can be viewed as language-specific options. There is, however, substantial evidence that human listeners can make effective use of prelexical representations, of one kind or another.

H. Conclusion

The questions currently at issue in the study of human speech recognition concern the relationship between the output of the auditory preprocessor and the input to the lexicon. How can auditory features be extracted from the parallel auditory stream; how can such a representation in terms of auditory featuresbe segmented for presentation to the lexicon; how can it be transformed into a more abstract form corresponding to stored representations; does the transformation process necessarily imply an intermediate level of prelexical representation; and if so, in what order do segmentation and transformation occur?

Up till the present time these questions have not been the most central in psycholinguistics. They have been comparatively neglected simply because of the separation of psycholinguistic terms of reference from those of auditory processing. Only the rapid growth of research on automatic speech recognition has encouraged psycholinguists to address these issues, because they must be resolved before the degree of relevance of human recognition evidence to the design of automatic recognisers can be determined.

However, the possibility of language-specificity at this level of processing is a dimension which should not be ignored. It is likely that psycholinguistic work will in the future become more cross-linguistic, i.e. will look at auditory word recognition and the segmentation and representational unit questions in the light of the ways in which languages differ. Such factors as presence versus absence of stress, relative occurrence of vowel reduction, frequency of prefixing versus suffixing, occurrence of stem-initial phoneme mutation, and phonetic functions of the prosodic dimensions of pitch, intensity and duration are all factors relevant to prelexical speech processing. It is at this level that the contrast between the psychoacoustic and the psycholinguistic approaches becomes particularly apparent. Psychoacousticians must be justified in assuming that the human auditory system is the same for everyone, and that the output of auditory preprocessing is the same kind of representation for all languages. Psycholinguists can no longer assume that the prelexical transformation process is the same for everyone, or that its output, i.e. the lexical input representation, is the same for all languages. Nonetheless, psycholinguists' new awareness of the transformation from auditory features as a central problem in speech recognition suggests that we may soon be seeing co-operative research projects addressing human speech recognition from the first auditory percept all the way to the lexicon. Such projects should, we suggest, also be of enormous value to engineers working on automatic speech recognition. In Part 3 we suggest some techniques which might be exploited by this new research axis.

3. CONVERTING THE AUDITORY STREAM INTO A PHONETIC CODE

This part of the paper outlines three current engineering approaches to the problem of converting the parallel data stream flowing from the auditory system into a sequence of discrete speech events. In each case, the acoustic input is subjected to a spectral analysis like that of the spectrogram and the resulting data stream is used as a substitute for auditory analysis. The frequency dimension is divided into channels and the number of channels varies from around 20 in vocoder style front-ends to 128 or 256 in the case of FFT-based front-ends. The temporal dimension is divided into time bins, or frames, which vary in duration from around 10 to 40 ms. The methods for generating the spectral representation vary considerably, but in each case, the data rate is relatively low and the temporal resolution is coarse in comparison with that of the auditory system. A detailed description of the techniques is presented in Bristow (1986); the current description is primarily concerned with how each approach tackles the problem of segmenting the parallel auditory stream into a discrete stream of phonological units, and to what extent each approach can capture cognitive psychological distinctions.

A. Feature Extraction

The traditional signal processing approach is based on the concept of feature extraction. Each frame of the spectrogram is searched for concentrations of energy, and adjacent frames are compared to establish the temporal and spectral extent of these auditory events. The events form patterns referred to as auditory featureswhich are often characteristic of the sound source. A subset of the auditory features that appear in the spectrogram represent speech events. For example, the pattern of formants that represent the [ae] in "past" and the burst of noise that represents the [s] in "past" (see Figure 1), are both examples of auditory features which are also speech events. In feature extraction models, the recognition system uses the features to establish the presence of phonemes, or other phonological units; then from this discrete stream of phonological units is generated a restricted list of word candidates with associated probabilities. Examples of different approaches to the feature extraction technique are provided by Assmann and Summerfield (1986), Duncan, Dalby and Jack (1986) and Lindsey, Johnson and Fourcin, (1986).

One of the main problems with the feature extraction approach is that it offers no particular solution to the segmentation problem. As we saw above, boundaries between units at all levels of analysis can be very unclear. There is no obvious cue either in the acoustic stream or in the auditory stream to signal where one lexical unit ends and the next begins; and the same is true of prelexical units. A portion of the signal which psycholinguists, and listeners, would unhesitatingly classify as containing two distinct phonemes, for instance, might offer no such clear contrast in terms of auditory features. As an example, a prevocalic stop consonant can appear more as a modification of the vowel that follows it than as a distinct auditory feature. Thus in the feature extraction approach the processes of extracting the features and of segmenting the continuous signal interact, and the approach therefore does not lend itself to a separation of levels of processing such as we have argued must be characteristic of human speech recognition.

B. Template Matching

In this technique, instead of each frame of the auditory stream being analysed separately, the frames are analysed in groups to see if the group contains a pattern that is characteristic of a speech event. It is a pattern recognition process in which the pattern in the group of frames is compared to each member of a set of canonical patterns, or templates. In fact the templates usually correspond to words, and so the template that provides the best match identifies the word candidate without the need of any intervening level of representation.

Template-matching approaches vary in sophistication from those which seek an exact match for untransformed stretches of speech to those which can cope to some extent with variability. The most successful technique at this time is Hidden Markov Modelling (HMM) and most current commercial devices use some form of it (Moore, 1986). It is a statistical pattern-recognition technique for modelling time-varying sequences and as such is particularly appropriate for speech. Each "template" is an HMM and each has to be learned. That is, the machine is trained on a range of forms that a word can take, and the HMM of that word is then a template that attempts to capture the variability of the word as well as its average form.

Template matching solves part of the segmentation problem inasmuch as the templates span whole sequences of what would be separate featuresin the previous technique. As a result, segmentation at the prelexical level does not arise, and the problem of segmentation is restricted to the level of the word-size template. The template has to be aligned with the part of the auditory stream to which it is being compared, and then it has to be stretched or compressed in time to fit the sample. The combined process takes a considerable amount of computation, and so, indirectly, segmentation remains an area where improvements are required (Cook and Russell, 1986).

The fact that a template is required for each word to be recognised means that there are far more primitive units in this system than there are in a feature-extracting system. And the fact that each template has to be compared with each input sample as it comes along means that a recognition machine based on this technique requires considerable computer power if it is to operate in real time. Nevertheless, the technique provides impressive performance when compared to its predecessors.

C. Learning Machines

The final technique is connectionism, or neural networking. The technique arose in cognitive science as a development of learning-machine research. Recently, it has been introduced into speech recognition as a means of converting the auditory stream into a phonetic stream (Bridle and Moore, 1984). At the same time it has captured the attention of psycholinguists as a useful framework for modelling human recognition performance (McClelland & Elman, 1986). In essence, a connectionist model is set up to learn the relationships between auditory patterns and phonetic codes. Many simple calculation units are set out in layers and each unit in one layer is connected to all of the units in the next layer by weighted links. Typically, units are connected to other units in the same layer only by mutually inhibitory links. In the case of speech recognition, the model usually has three layers of units: input units which characterise the auditory possibilities, output units which characterise the phonetic possibilities, and hidden units which connect the input and output units and make it possible for the model to learn complex relationships between the input and output states. The models are trained, as one would expect, by presenting the auditory patterns associated with words to the input units, the phonetic representations of the words to the output units, and adjusting the weights that connect the units to provide the "best fit" (Elman and Zipser, 1987; Landauer, Kamm and Singhal, 1987; Peeling and Bridle, 1986; Prager and Fallside, 1989).

The computation time taken to learn the relationship between a relatively modest set of auditory and phonetic events is currently astronomical: hours on a large mainframe computer and days on a workstation. However, once the network has learned the items, it can provide a phonetic transcription for an auditory pattern reasonably quickly. Part of the reason is that the network does not compare the input to all possible outputs sequentially. The memory in the network is contained in the set of weights derived in the learning session, and that one set of weights is used to convert all inputs to all outputs. The advantage of these machines, then, is that they effectively compare the input pattern to all of the stored representations simultaneously.

connectionist models have had similar problems to HMM models with respect to segmenting the auditory stream and scaling the stream temporally. In one recent model, Waibel et al. (1987) attempt to solve part of this problem by expanding the input-unit layer to include several copies of the current auditory input. It increases the architectural complexity and the computational load considerably but it does make the model more resistant to temporal variation. Very recently there have also been attempts to explore connectionist architectures which are specifically adapted to dealing with temporal information, for instance dynamic nets (e.g. Norris, 1988). These approaches will probably produce the next generation of connectionist recognition systems.

It remains to be seen whether this approach will lead to better performance than the HMM approach. connectionist modelling, does, however, illustrate how cognitive science is being extended into the realm of peripheral auditory processing. Importantly, it is also the first modelling framework to gain equal popularity with speech engineers and cognitive psychologists. Thus it offers, for the first time, a ready-made framework within which constraints derived from our knowledge of human recognition performance can be applied to the design of an ASR system.

CONCLUSION

In this paper we have described current work on the psychological modelling of auditory processing and word recognition. We have also briefly discussed available methods for connecting the auditory and speech systems, all of which now leads us to argue for a particular approach to the study of speech recognition, one which we believe offers the best chance currently available for new progress in the design of a general purpose automatic speech recogniser.

We have made two distinct claims. Firstly, we have argued that ASR research should make use of the resources offered by cognitive psychology. Although we do not yet understand human speech processing in sufficient detail to model the system both accurately and completely, we do understand a number of the constraints which apply to human processing, and in particular we know a great deal about the distinct levels of processing involved. The human speech recognition system demonstrates that real-time speaker-independent large-vocabulary recognition is possible. In the long term, therefore, the human system is both the standard which ASR seeks to emulate and, we would argue, the best model it can hope to adopt.

Our second argument concerns the relationship between areas within cognitive psychology. Traditionally psychoacoustic studies of auditory processing and psycholinguistic studies of speech recognition have been independent and non-interacting disciplines. We believe that if cognitive psychology is to make a useful contribution to ASR research, cognitive psychologists first have to achieve an integrated model of human speech recognition which covers all aspects of the process from initial processing of the incoming waveform to successful location of stored representations of words. This means that psychoacousticians have to consider the nature of their model's output representation, and how such a representation might be constrained by the nature of subsequent processing; and it means that psycholinguists have to consider likewise the nature of their model's input representation, and how this can be translated into the discrete units required by the word recognition system

In the main body of the chapter we have argued that cognitive psychological modelling is relevant to ASR research, and that collaboration between psychoacousticians and psycholinguists is feasible. In Part 3 we suggest that at the present time one type of methodology presents the best opportunity for progress. connectionist modelling offers the prospect of uniting psychologists and engineers because it is a technique which is currently proving useful in both fields. It is also explicitly based, in a sense, on the human system in that the design of connectionist networks is intended to mimic the relationship between groups of neurons in the brain. We should make it clear, of course, that we do not consider this aspect of connectionist methodology to be central to its value; it is by no means necessary that a connectionist model is *ipso facto* a model of the human system. What we consider important in the present context is the computational power of connectionist systems, as well as the fact that they are adaptable both to cognitive modelling and to engineering design.

Current connectionist models of speech recognition, however, are implausible models of human processing. Consider the top part of Figure 8, which represents a typical current model. It has two stages: the first converts the incoming waveform into an auditory representation in terms of a spectrogram; the second is a giant undifferentiated connectionist model which attempts to associate spectral representations with words. As we have argued above, the spectrogram does not even approach the level of fine-grain analysis which the human auditory system applies to incoming waveforms. And as we have also argued, the conversion of auditory features to lexical representations in the human recognition system is not an undifferentiated process, but consists of a number of separable processing levels.

We propose, therefore, that the connectionist modelling required for the next generation of recognition machines should be more like the bottom half of Figure 8. Firstly, instead of relying on a poor-definition spectrogram, the system should simulate the human auditory system, mimicking first the processing which is performed by the cochlea, then the processing performed by the neural auditory system. Secondly, the conversion of auditory features to lexical representations should not be attempted in one stage; rather it should proceed in isolatable stages, involving intermediate levels of representation prior to lexical access.

This proposal does not, of course, constitute a complete and detailed model of the human system. For instance, the figure is explicitly neutral with respect to the nature

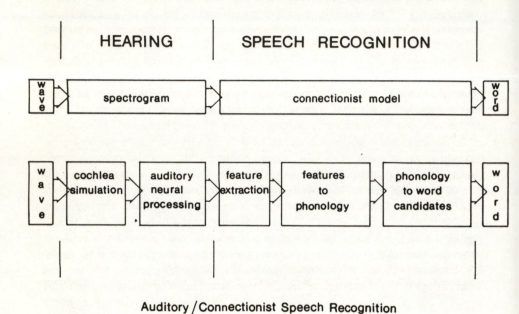

Auditory/Connectionist Speech Recognition

FIG. 3.8   A comparison of existing (upper row) and proposed (lower row) methods of word recognition using the auditory/connectionist approach. The spectrogram in the upper row is replaced by a full cochlea simulation and a pulse ribbon model of auditory neural processing in the lower row. The monolithic connectionist model in the upper row is replaced by a psychological, staged model in which features are extracted from the auditory image and converted into a sublexical form of phonology before the phonology is assembled into word candidates.

of prelexical representations (phonemes, demisyllables and syllables are among the possibilities here). It is not the processing details that we are arguing for; it is the general structure of the model. We believe that this general structure is the right choice for the next generation of speech recognition models.

ACKNOWLEDGEMENTS

The implementation of the gammatone filterbank, and the software used to produce the figures in the paper, were both developed by John Holdsworth.

REFERENCES

Aitchison, J. (1987) *Words in the Mind: An Introduction to the Mental Lexicon.* Oxford: Blackwell.

Assmann, P. & Summerfield, Q. (1986) Modelling the perception of concurrent vowels. *Proceedings of the Institute of Acoustics: Speech and Hearing,* Vol. 8, Part 7, 53-60.

Beet, S.W., Moore, R.K. and Tomlinson, M.J. (1986) Auditory modelling for automatic speech recognition. *Proceedings of the Institute of Acoustics: Speech and Hearing,* Vol. 8, Part 7, 571-580.

Békésy, G. von (1960) *Experiments in Hearing.* New York: McGraw Hill.

Bridle, J.S. & Moore, R.K. (1984) Boltzmann machines for speech pattern processing. *Proceedings of the Institute of Acoustics,* Vol. 6, Part 4, 315-322.

Bristow, G. (Ed.) (1986) *Electronic Speech Recognition.* London: Collins.

Carlson, R., Granström, B., and Klatt, D. (1980) Vowel perception: The relative perceptual salience of selected acoustic manipulations, *Speech Transmission Laboratory Quarterly Progress and Status Report* (TRITA-TLF-79-4), Stockholm, Sweden, 73-83.

Cook, A.E. and Russell, M.J. (1986) Improved duration modelling in hidden Markeov models using series-parallel configuration of states. *Proceedings of the Institute of Acoustics: Speech and Hearing,* Vol. 8, Part 7, 299-307.

Cooke, M.P. (1986) Towards an early symbolic representation of speech based on auditory modelling. *Proceedings of the Institute of Acoustics: Speech and Hearing,* Vol. 8, Part 7, 563-570.

Cutler, A. (1985) Cross-language psycholinguistics. *Linguistics,* 23, 659-667.

Cutler, A., Mehler, J., Norris, D. & Segui, J. (1986) The syllable's differing role in the segmentation of French and English. *Journal of Memory and Language,* 25, 385-400.

de Boer, E. & de Jongh, H.R. (1978) On cochlear encoding: Potentialities and limitations of the reverse correlation technique. *Journal of the Acoustical Society of America,* 63, 115-135.

de Boer, E. (1983) No sharpening? A challenge for cochlear mechanics. *Journal of the Acoustical Society of America,* 73, (2), 567-573.

Delgutte, B. (1980) Representation of speechlike sounds in the discharge patterns of auditory-nerve fibers. *Journal of the Acoustical Society of America,* 68, 843.

Dolmazon, J.M. (1982): Representation of speech-like sounds in the peripheral auditory system in light of a model. In R. Carlson and B. Granström, (Eds.) *The Representation of Speech in the Peripheral Auditory System.* Amsterdam: Elsevier; 151-163.

Duncan, G., Dalby, J. & Jack, M.A. (1986) Star-pak: A signal processing package for acoustic phonetic analysis of speech. *Proceedings of the Institute of Acoustics: Speech and Hearing,* Vol. 8, Part 7, 77-84.

Elman, J.L. & Zipser, D. (1987) Learning the hidden structure of speech. Institute for Cognitive Science, UCSD, California Report 8701.

Friederici, A.D. & Schoenle, P.W. (1980) Computational dissociation of two vocabulary types: Evidence from aphasia. *Neuropsychologia,* 18, 11-20.

Fujimura, O. & Lovins, J.B. (1978) Syllables as concatenative phonetic units. In A. Bell & J.B. Hooper (Eds.) *Syllables and Segments.* Amsterdam: North-Holland.

Fujimura, O. & Lovins, J.B. (1982) *Syllables as concatenative phonetic units.* Indiana University Linguistics Club.

Gardner, R.B. and Uppal, M.K. (1986) A peripheral auditory model for speech processing. *Proceedings of the Institute of Acoustics: Speech and Hearing,* Vol. 8, Part 7, 555-562.

Ghitza, O. (1986): Auditory nerve representation as a front-end for speech recognition in a noisy environment. *Computer Speech & Language,* 2, 109-130.

Goldstein, J.L. (1973) An optimum processor theory for the central formation of the pitch of complex tones. *Journal of the Acoustical Society of America,* 54, 1496-1516.

Goldstein, J.L. & Srulovicz, P. (1977) Auditory-nerve spike intervals as an adequate basis for aural frequency measurement. In E.F. Evans and J.P. Wilson (Eds.) *Psychophysics and Physiology of Hearing.* Academic Press: New York.

Helmholtz, H.L.F., von (1875, 1912) *On the Sensations of Tone*. English translation of 4th edition by A.J. Ellis (Longmans, Green and Co., London, 1912).

Henderson, L. (Ed.) (1984) *Orthographies and Reading*. London: Erlbaum.

Houtgast, T. (1974) Lateral suppression in hearing. Thesis, Free University of Amsterdam, Academische Pers. BV, Amsterdam.

Hunt, M.J. & Lefebvre, C. (1987): Speech recognition using an auditory model with pitch-synchronous analysis. *Proceedings of the IEEE International Conference on Acoustics, Speech and Signal Processing, ICASSP-87*, Dallas, 813-816.

Johannesma, P.I.M. (1972) The pre-response stimulus ensemble of neurons in the cochlear nucleus. *Proceedings Symposium on Hearing Theory*, pp.58-69. IPO, Eindhoven, The Netherlands.

Jusczyk, P.W. (1986) A review of speech perception research. In K.R. Boff, L. Kaufman, & J.P. Thomas (Eds.) *Handbook of Perception and Human Performance*. New York: Wiley.

Klatt, D.H. (1979) Speech perception: A model of acoustic-phonetic analysis and lexical access. *Journal of Phonetics*, 7, 279-312.

Landauer, T.K., Kamm, C.A. & Singhal, S. (1987) Teaching a minimally structured back-propagation network to recognise speech sounds. Bell Communications Research Report.

Lindsey, G., Johnson, M. & Fourcin, A. (1986) Diminution of high frequency energy as a cue to the voicelessness of following consonants. *Proceedings of the Institute of Acoustics: Speech and Hearing*, Vol. 8, Part 7, 25-30.

Lyon, R.F. (1984) Computational models of neural auditory processing. *Proceedings IEEE International Conference on Acoustics, Speech and Signal Processing* (March), paper 36.1.

Marslen-Wilson, W.D. (1980) Speech understanding as a psychological process. In J.D. Simon (Ed.) *Spoken Language Generation and Recognition*. Dordrecht: Reidel.

Mathes, R.C. & Miller, R.L. (1947). Phase effects in monaural perception. *Journal of the Acoustical Society of America, 18*, 780-797

McClelland, J.L. & Elman, J.L. (1986) The TRACE model of speech perception. *Cognitive Psychology*, 18, 1-86.

Meddis, R. (1986) Simulation of mechanical to neural transduction in the auditory receptor. *Journal of the Acoustical Society of America, 79*, 702-711.

Mehler, J. (1981) The role of syllables in speech processing. *Philosophical Transactions of the Royal Society*, B295, 333-352.

Moore, B.C.J. & Glasberg, B.R. (1983). Suggested formulae for calculating auditory-filter bandwidths and excitation patterns. *Journal of the Acoustical Society of America, 74*, 750-753

Moore, R.K. (1986) Computational techniques. *Electronic Speech Recognition*, G. Bristow (Ed.), London: Collins, 130-157.

Norris, D.G. (1988) A dynamic net model of speech recognition. Paper presented to Workshop on Computational and Cognitive Approaches to Speech Processing. Sperlonga, Italy.

Norris, D.G. and Cutler, A. (1988) The relative accessibility of phonemes and syllables. *Perception & Psychophysics, 43*, 541-550.

Patterson, R.D. (1973) The effects of relative phase and the number of components on residue pitch. *Journal of the Acoustical Society of America, 53*, 1565-1572.

Patterson, R.D. (1976) Auditory filter shapes derived with noise stimuli. *Journal of the Acoustical Society of America, 67*, 229-245.

Patterson, R.D. (1986) Spiral detection of periodicity and the spiral form of musical scales. *Psychology of Music, 14*, 44-61.

Patterson, R.D. (1987a) A pulse ribbon model of peripheral auditory processing. In William A. Yost and Charles, S. Watson, (Eds.) *Auditory Processing of Complex Sounds*. Hillsdale, N.J.: Erlbaum, 167-179.

Patterson, R.D. (1987b) A pulse ribbon model of monaural phase perception. *Journal of the Acoustical Society of America, 82*, (5), 1560-1586.

Patterson, R.D. and Moore, B.C.J. (1986) Auditory filters and excitation patterns as representations of frequency resolution. In B.C.J. Moore (Ed.) *Frequency Selectivity in Hearing*. Academic: London,

123-177.

Patterson, R.D. Nimmo-Smith, I. Weber, D.L. & Milroy, R. (1982) The deterioration of hearing with age: Frequency selectivity, the critical ratio, the audiogram, and speech threshold. *Journal of the Acoustical Society of America, 72*, 1788-1803.

Patterson, R.D. and Wightman, F.L. (1976) Residue pitch as a function of component spacing. *Journal of the Acoustical Society of America, 59*, 1450-1459.

Peeling, S. & Bridle, J. (1986) Experiments with a learning network for a simple phonetic task. *Proceedings of the Institute of Acoustics: Speech and Hearing*, Vol. 8, Part 7, 315-322.

Perkell, J.S. & Klatt, D.H. (1986) *Invariance and Variability in Speech Processes*. Hillsdale, N.J.: Erlbaum.

Pisoni, D.B. (1981) Phonetic representations and lexical access. Paper presented to the Acoustical Society of America, Ottawa, May; (*Journal of the Acoustical Society of America, 69*, 532).

Pisoni, D.B. & Luce, P.A. (1986). Speech perception: Research, theory, and the principal issues. In E.C. Schwab & H.C. Nusbaum (Eds.) *Pattern Recognition by Humans and Machines*. Vol. 1. New York: Academic Press.

Pisoni, D.B., Nusbaum, H.C., Luce, P.A. & Slowiaczek, L.M. (1985) Speech perception, word recognition and the structure of the lexicon. *Speech Communication, 4*, 75-95.

Prager, R.W. & Fallside, F. (1989). The modified Kanerva model for automatic speech recognition. *Computer Speech and Language, 3*, 61-81.

Schofield, D. (1985) Visualisations of speech based on a model of the peripheral auditory system. NPL Report DITC 62/85.

Schwid, H.A., & Geisler, C.D. (1982). "Multiple Reservoir Model of Neurotransmitter Release by a Cochlear Inner Hair Cell", *Journal of the Acoustical Society of America, 72*, 1435-1440.

Seashore, R.H. & Eckerson, L.D. (1940) The measurement of individual differences in general English vocabularies. *Journal of Educational Psychology, 31*, 14-38.

Segui, J. (1984) The syllable: A basic perceptual unit in speech processing. In H. Bouma & D.G. Bouwhuis (Eds.) *Attention and Performance X*. Hillsdale, N.J.: Erlbaum.

Seneff, S. (1984) Pitch and spectral estimation of speech based on auditory synchrony model, *Proceedings of the IEEE International Conference on Acoustics, Speech and Signal Processing*, San Diego, (March), paper 36.2, vol. 3.

Shamma, S.A. (1986) Encoding the acoustic spectrum in the spatio-temporal responses of the auditory nerve. In B.C.J. Moore and R.D. Patterson (Eds.) *Auditory Frequency Selectivity*. Plenum: New York, 289-298.

Swinney, D.A. and Cutler, A. (1979) The access and processing of idiomatic expressions. *Journal of Verbal Learning and Verbal Behavior, 18*, 523-534.

Taft, M. (1988) A morphological decomposition model of lexical representation. *Linguistics, 26*, 657-668

Terhardt, E. (1974) Pitch, consonance and harmony. *Journal of the Acoustical Society of America, 55*, 1061-1069.

Tranmuller, H. (1987) Phase vowels. In M.E.H. Schouten (Ed.). *The Psychophysics of Speech Perception*. Dordrecht: Martinus Nijhoff.

Van Lancker, D. (1975) Heterogeneity in language and speech: Neurolinguistic studies. *UCLA Working Papers in Phonetics, 29*.

Waibel, A., Hanazawa, T., Hinton, G., Shikano, K. & Lang, K. (1987) Phoneme recognition using time-delay neural networks, ATR Technical Report TR-1-0006.

Wakefield, G.H. (1987) Detection of envelope phase disparity. *Journal of the Acoustical Society of America, 81*, Suppl. 1, S34.

Wegel, R.L. and Lane, C.E. (1924) The auditory masking of one sound by another and its probable relation to the dynamics of the inner ear. *Physiological Review, 23*, 266-285.

Wightman, F.L. (1973) The pattern transformation model of pitch. *Journal of the Acoustical Society of America, 54*, 407-416.

Yost, W.A. and Watson, C.S. (1987) *Auditory Processing of Complex Sounds*. Hillsdale, N.J.: Erlbaum.

Young, E.D. and Sachs, M.B. (1979) Representation of steady-state vowels in the temporal aspects of the discharge patterns of populations of auditory-nerve fibers. *Journal of the Acoustical Society of America*, *66*, 1381-1403.

CHAPTER 4

Learning and Memory

W. A. Phillips

Centre for Cognitive and Computational Neuroscience,
Department of Psychology, Stirling, Scotland.

A. D. Baddeley

MRC Applied Psychology Unit, 15 Chaucer Road,
Cambridge, CB2 2EF, England.

1. INTRODUCTION

The capacity to learn and remember is perhaps the most central feature of human cognition. An individual who was born without the capacity to see, to hear or to understand language would truly be handicapped, but an individual with no capacity to learn or remember would be devastated, reduced to the level of a vegetable. The process of learning is clearly one of enormous importance, and for that if no other reason, understanding how we learn and remember is of great significance, and over the years has generated a number of contrasting approaches. The last few years has seen the development of great interest in a particular approach to modelling learning and memory that is sometimes referred to as connectionism, or the parallel distributed processing (PDP) approach to memory. Since this is one of the most active and exciting current areas of cognitive science, we felt that this should feature prominently in a chapter on learning and memory. For that reason, one of us (W.A.P.) was invited to write the relevant chapter. During the discussion that preceded the writing of the chapter, members of the cognitive group felt that it was important to place such developments within a broader context, and the second of us (A.D.B.) agreed to undertake this. The chapter that follows therefore comprises two major sections, the first written by A.D.B. and the second by W.A.P.; we regard them as complementary. The area of learning and memory is however very extensive, and any attempt to cover it within a single brief chapter will necessarily be incomplete, and tend to reflect those

61

areas the authors themselves find particularly interesting and feel able to cover. While one of these, machine learning, has been briefly covered in a section by Richard Young, many other important topics such as classical and instrumental conditioning, work on the development of memory, memory for faces or skill acquisition are regretfully omitted.

2. THE PSYCHOLOGY OF LEARNING AND MEMORY: AN OVERVIEW

2.1 The Nature of the Problem

At one level, the problem is very clear; learning involves the acquisition and storage of information, and memory its subsequent maintenance and retrieval. One simply needs to know what the basic units of learning are, perhaps links or associations, and then study the way in which such associations are combined to form habits, skills, and networks of knowledge.

This approach was favoured by associationist philosophers, and by a range of psychological theorists. Such approaches have, however, had relatively little success in providing adequate explanations for the rich and varied phenomena of human memory. There may indeed prove to be atomic units that underlie all learning and memory, but so far they have not been isolated. Furthermore, if they were, we would still be left with many problems as to how such basic units combine; we would be like architects who knew about bricklaying, but nothing about the principles of architectural design. Indeed, the connectionist approach would suggest that it is fundamentally misguided to attempt to study single associations, since the process of learning consists in changing patterns of associations among many interacting subcomponents.

Suppose then that we start at the other end of the problem. Instead of postulating basic atomic units of learning, let us look at the range of phenomena of learning and memory that we want to explain. The problem here is the sheer complexity of the manifestations of memory. Suppose we begin with a simple practical situation. A local hospital makes a practice of teaching all incoming staff about the dangers of damaging their backs and gives instruction in methods for lifting patients. What might student nurses attending this course be expected to learn? First of all, they might be told something about the anatomy of the back, and the biomechanics of lifting. Secondly, they would be taught the skill of lifting, something which they would probably need to practice before acquiring. Thirdly, they might absorb some attitude about the importance of taking care to lift appropriately. Subsequently, as a result of this, and one hopes of supervision by and imitation of senior colleagues, they may develop the habit of always lifting in an appropriate way. Finally, when questioned a few years later, they may or may not be able to recollect the initial classes on lifting, who had taught them, what the surroundings were, and so forth.

Note that each of these aspects of learning is potentially separable. A student could give a very good account of the anatomy of the back, and yet fail to be able to demonstrate a lift, or be able to lift, but habitually not do so. He or she could perhaps subsequently remember the occasion of the initial course in some detail, while having forgotten all of its contents. It is therefore at least plausible that learning involves not one, but many different processes.

In the past, attempts to study learning and memory have tended to focus on one or two paradigmatic situations, largely ignoring the rest, although in recent years there has been much more concern with the attempt to fractionate human memory into subsystems and components. We will therefore attempt to give a broad overview by considering very briefly some of the diverse approaches to the study of learning before going on to outline more recent work on the fractionation of memory.

2.2 Neurobiological Approaches

These are primarily concerned with the physical basis of memory including problems of the localisation of memory within the brain, and with the physiological and neurochemical changes that accompany learning. For obvious reasons, neurobiologists have typically worked with animals, often using the acquisition of simple habits connected with the avoidance of shock or acquisition of a reward. In the past, the link with cognitive science in general and cognitive psychology in particular has been weak. This is, however, beginning to change with the growing interest in the interpretation of the dementias in neurochemical terms. This has led to a concern with attempting to bridge the gap between animal models and human behaviour, resulting in a healthy increase in collaborative work (see Kopelman, 1986, for a review). The development of the connectionist models (described later) is another factor that is likely to lead to an increased link between cognitive psychology and neurobiology.

Learning Theory

During the 1940s and 1950s the attempt to find general principles of learning was perhaps the most vigorous area of theoretical activity, particularly in North American psychology. The work was principally based on animal models and included the research of such figures as Hull, Tolman, Guthrie, and Skinner. In the late 1950s it suddenly fell from fashion, largely because of the difficulty it appeared to have in explaining more complex aspects of behaviour. It was followed by an increasing concern with human memory and learning, initially based on simple stimulus response associationist models, but during the 1960s it was increasingly influenced by computer models and the information-processing approach.

Two aspects of this earlier behavioural tradition have continued to be active. The first stems from the work of Skinner, where the technology of operant conditioning has been applied with some success. A parallel development stemming from the classical conditioning tradition has produced the behaviour therapy approach to the treatment of anxiety disorders (an overview is given in Wilson, Franks, Brownell, & Kendall, 1984).

While the Skinnerian approach does not seem to have led to a particularly rich theoretical development, other less atheoretical approaches have attempted to generate general principles of learning using animal models. This approach is typified by researchers such as Rescorla and Wagner in the U.S. and Mackintosh and his co-workers in Europe (see Nilsson & Archer, 1985). The concepts and techniques of human cognitive psychology have increasingly influenced animal research, but the flow of ideas in the other direction has so far been relatively limited. Once again, there appear to be some signs that connectionism may offer a potential bridge. More specifically, some of the learning principles postulated by Rescorla and Wagner to account for conditioning in animals prove to be very similar to the rules assumed by certain connectionist models which attempt to account for human learning. Attempts to apply these principles to human subjects in relatively complex tasks such as those simulating medical decision-making appear promising (Gluck & Bower, 1988).

2.3 Computer Science

This has influenced the study of memory in a number of ways. First of all, it has provided a series of metaphors that have underpinned the information-processing approach to memory. Secondly, it has given rise to a number of models that were expressed in the terms of computer programs, ranging from early models such as Feigenbaum and Simon's EPAM through to John Anderson's latest model ACT*. Such models have continued to be widely acknowledged, and in some areas very influential. However, models of this complexity demand a great deal of commitment from the potential user; we suspect that many people in the field are simply unable or unwilling to provide this commitment, exposing models to the danger of being regarded as monuments rather than theoretical tools. This is a real problem in cognitive science, where complex models are perhaps inevitable.

One program which has had a broad influence on cognitive psychology is Quillian's Teachable Language Comprehender, which included an attempted simulation of semantic memory (Quillian, 1969). The feature of this model of knowledge representation that caused more attention was its hierarchical storage assumption, together with the principle of economy, whereby features that were characteristic of a whole set of things were stored at the higher nodes within the hierarchy and retrieved by moving up the network. In fact, the experimental demonstration of this effect did not prove robust (Conrad, 1972), but other ideas incorporated within the model, such as that of spreading activation, have continued to be very influential (cf. Collins & Loftus, 1975).

While Quillian's work was important in confronting cognitive psychologists with the need to model the acquisition and retrieval of knowledge, the various attempts to produce semantic memory models during the 1970s were not conspicuously successful, and tend to have petered out (see Kintsch, 1980, for a review). Exceptions to this are Schank's work developing computer-based representations of the social context and knowledge underlying much of our comprehension of the world around us, and Kintsch's work on language comprehension, both of which have continued to be productive (e.g. Schank, 1982; Kintsch & van Dijk, 1978). One might also describe some of the current parallel distributed processing models, such as those of Rumelhart and McClelland, as a direct evolution of earlier attempts to model semantic memory.

2.4 Neuropsychology

Classically, neuropsychology has been concerned with the relationship between brain localisation and function. In recent years, neuropsychology has become increasingly involved in using the breakdown of a particular function as a means of understanding the normal operation of the system (this issue is discussed in more detail by Vallar in Volume Four). The link with cognitive psychology has of recent years been particularly fruitful, and will be discussed in more detail below.

2.5 Cognitive Psychology

Research on human memory has formed one of the most active areas of cognitive psychology over the last 20 years. The strength of such work is that it has successfully identified a range of phenomena and come up with a number of broad general principles. These include observations on conditions under which distributed practice is better than massed, on the role of organisation in learning, on the conceptual distinction between encoding, storage and retrieval, and on such determinants of retrieval as the encoding specificity principle (see Baddeley, in press and Crowder, 1976 for reviews of this literature).

Any attempt to model human memory must be able to account for this rich body of data. One weakness of this approach, however, is that a great deal of the data is based on relatively standard laboratory paradigms in which the subject is presented with a set of material, usually lists of words, and recalls them shortly afterwards. There is no doubt that this paradigm catches some important aspects of human memory, but it is far from clear just to what extent the principles that apply within such situations can be generalised (Neisser, 1978; 1981).

One area of research in cognitive psychology that is particularly relevant to this latter point stems from the attempts to fractionate memory into subcomponents, an area of research in which cognitive psychology and neuropsychology have proved to be productive allies.

3. THE FRACTIONATION OF HUMAN MEMORY

As early as the 1940s, Hebb (1949) suggested the need to assume separable long- and short-term memory systems. The topic remained dormant, however, until the late 1950s when the development of short-term memory paradigms revived the question and led to considerable activity in the 1960s aimed at deciding between a unitary view of memory, typically advocated by those with a stimulus response associationist view of long-term memory, and a dichotomous view. During the mid-1960s, evidence began to accumulate suggesting the need to assume two kinds of memory. This included the observation that certain standard memory tasks appeared to have two components—a durable long-term component and a more labile, possibly short-term component (Glanzer & Cunitz, 1966). In the case of verbal memory, the evidence seemed to indicate that the immediate recall of unrelated lists of words depended on remembering their sound, whereas long-term learning was much more dependent on their meaning (Baddeley, 1966a; 1966b). Finally, evidence from neuropsychological patients suggested a double dissociation between long- and short-term memory. Patients suffering from the classic amnesic syndrome show a dramatic incapacity to acquire new material, together with an unimpaired capacity to perform certain short-term memory tasks, such as the immediate recall of a string of numbers (Milner, 1966); conversely, other patients showed grossly impaired immediate memory for auditory material, coupled with normal long-term learning ability (Shallice & Warrington, 1970). By the late 1960s, the evidence for a dual memory store appeared very strong, and a range of dichotomous models appeared, of which the most influential was that of Atkinson and Shiffrin (1968).

During the 1970s, however, the apparent consensus started to break down as inconsistencies began to appear in the evidence that had previously seemed unequivocal. This led to two further developments, the first being the *Levels of Processing* approach of Craik and Lockhart (1972). This moved away from the assumption of separate types of memory, concentrating on the role of coding in trace durability. It suggested the simple generalisation that the more deeply and richly an item was encoded, the more durably will it be stored. This stimulated a great deal of research during the 1970s, and has proved to be a useful rule of thumb, but has proved rather less fruitful in generating further theoretical development.

The second development was the exploration by Baddeley and Hitch (1974) of the concept of*Working Memory,* a system assumed to act as a temporary store playing a crucial role in such cognitive skills as learning, reasoning, and understanding. This research began with the assumption of a short-term store as suggested by the standard dichotomous memory view, but rapidly began to accumulate evidence that the assumption of a single monolithic short-term store was probably unjustified. It led to the concept of Working Memory as an alliance of subsystems comprising an attentional control system, the *Central Executive* aided by a number of slave systems. The most prominent of these were the *Articulatory Loop,* used for storing speech-based information, and the *Visuo-spatial Sketchpad,* a system for setting up and manipulating visual images. The system was intentionally not specified in great detail, but nevertheless has been fruitful over the years, not only in accounting for the standard data from the psychology laboratory, but also in fitting data from brain-damaged patients and in suggesting applications outside the laboratory. The model has, for example, so far been applied to reading and dyslexia, counting, to the measurement of workload, and to the analysis of senile dementia (Baddeley, 1986).

More recently, evidence has begun to accumulate that long-term memory itself is not a unitary system. The question of whether episodic memory, the recollection of personally-experienced events, involves the same system as semantic memory (acquisition and use of knowledge), or whether these reflect different uses of the same system, continues to be a point of considerable disagreement. This is well illustrated by Tulving (1984) and the associated peer review discussion.

A distinction that does appear to have more general support however is that between *procedural* or implicit learning and *declarative* or explicit learning. The distinction is shown most clearly in the case of amnesic patients who appear to combine a dramatic impairment in their capacity to acquire and recollect new information whether of a semantic or episodic type, while showing unimpaired performance on a wide range of other tasks (see Squire, 1982, for a review). One feature that seems to distinguish the preserved type of learning is that it does not require the patient to be aware of ever having encountered the material before. Hence amnesic patients can learn motor skills such as pursuit tracking, can be conditioned, can learn perceptual discriminations, or how to solve simple puzzles more rapidly. At the same time as they show clear evidence of learning, they are likely to deny ever having encountered these situations before. There appears, therefore, to be a distinction between a learning system that has been disrupted by the amnesia (declarative learning?) and a system that remains intact (procedural learning?). The deficit in amnesic patients appears to be associated typically with damage to the circuit linking the temporal lobes, hippocampi, mammillary bodies, and prefrontal cortex (Mishkin, 1982). The nature and distribution of the procedural learning process (if indeed it is a unitary process), is less well understood.

It would seem to be important for any complete cognitive model of memory to take account of the way in which human memory appears to be divided into subsystems which differ quite markedly in their characteristics. Any attempt to model human learning that ignores this diversity is unlikely to be satisfactory.

Interaction between cognitive psychology and neuropsychology continues to be lively and productive. It seems likely that the subcomponents of working memory will prove to be also components of systems that initially evolved in connection with more basic processes, such as speech perception and production, visual perception, and attentional control of action. In this respect, the boundary between research on memory and on perception and attention seem likely to become increasingly blurred. In the case of long-term memory, we clearly need to know a great deal more about procedural learning. At present it is defined largely in terms of a negative feature, the fact that it is not disturbed in the classic amnesic syndrome. It seems unlikely that all aspects of procedural learning, from classical conditioning through the acquisition of motor skills to learning complex intellectual skills, will prove to be based on the same system.

If we return to our original concern with specifying the range of human memory, we are I suspect forced to a similar conclusion. We almost certainly need a richer and more complex model of long-term memory if it is to capture the range of effects from acquiring habits and attitudes to remembering when to do something at a pre-set time, and from recalling events in our early lives to performing complex problem-solving skills. There has in the last decade been an increased willingness to attempt to study memory in the real world, despite its complexities. This has already begun to provide a fruitful stimulus to the development of concepts within the laboratory, and we expect this trend to continue and increase.

4. NEUROCOMPUTATIONAL STUDIES OF LEARNING AND MEMORY

So far this chapter has given an overview of the status and prospects of research on human learning and memory. This section deals with neurocomputational approaches which although still at a very early stage of development may be of relevance to cognitive psychology and to the focal concerns of this report. Neurocomputational theories involve the working hypothesis that the complex cognitive achievements of higher organisms are based upon the computational abilities that arise from the collective behaviour of large populations of simple processing elements. The study of such abilities is in its infancy. It involves formal analysis, modelling small nets on conventional or highly parallel computers, studying their dependence on parameters of biological significance, comparing their performance with that of normal and brain-damaged subjects, and with single unit activity in appropriate regions of neocortex. Computational theories with a neural interpretation are being studied in relation to language, problem solving, sensori-motor control, and early vision. Here we emphasise their relation to problems of learning and memory. Studies of machine learning have been important in artificial intelligence since at least Samuels' programs for playing checkers and improving their performance through learning. Such studies, in what could be called the "classical" AI tradition, are still developing healthily, and indeed have experienced a resurgence of vitality in the 1980s (see Michalski, Carbonell, & Mitchell, 1983; 1986, for surveys of the state of the art).

At present, the field is characterised by the exploration of a number of different-seeming mechanisms for learning, so that one finds work dealing with concept learning, rule learning, conceptual clustering, learning by generalisation, learning by analogy, and so on. Rather less effort is spent in attempting to understand how these apparently different techniques relate to one another, though for a good example of such work see Bundy, Silver, and Plummer (1985). The approaches also differ in how relevant they are to human cognition. Some of the computationally and memory-intensive techniques used for induction, which involve reprocessing entire collections of examples, would not seem to be immediately applicable to human learning. Other techniques are more so. One such technique of growing importance is known as "explanation-based learning", and is concerned with how one can learn significantly from a single example—a typically human capability. Silver (1986), for example, examining the ability to solve classes of algebraic and trigonometric equations, shows that one can learn a new transformation or solution method by analysing the role it plays in a worked example, in his case particularly by focussing on how the new step achieves the preconditions that make a previously known method applicable. Silver's work illustrates a kind of learning in which deliberate, knowledge-dependent cognition is brought to bear.

The most explicitly "psychological" learning mechanism studied is probably that of "learning by chunking". The term is used specifically of the work of Rosenbloom, Newell, and Laird (Rosenbloom & Newell, 1986; Laird, Rosenbloom, & Newell, 1986a) as embodied in the soar problem-solving architecture (Laird, Newell, & Rosenbloom, 1987; Newell, in prep.), but the approach is also closely similar to the theory of cognitive skill acquisition of Anderson (1986; 1987). The crucial ingredient is to couple learning to a model of problem solving which makes use of an explicit hierarchy of goals and subgoals. Chunking consists of storing a rule that records the result of the subgoal activity together with the conditions that gave rise to it, so that if the same situation is encountered again, the rule will apply and avoid the need to process the subgoal. The chunking mechanism is viewed not as an algorithm running on the architecture, but as a uniform, automatic, "syntactic" (i.e. knowledge-independent) property of the architecture itself. At first sight it might appear that such learning could hope only to repeat the original course of problem solving, albeit faster. But the work done with Soar shows that not to be the case. By making uniform use of subgoals to deal with all problems encountered by the mechanism (a principle known as "universal subgoaling": Laird, Rosenbloom, & Newell, 1986b), chunking gives rise to a wide variety of phenomena, including generalisation and the learning of new problem-solving operators and even new problem spaces (Newell, in prep.). At the present time, the limits of learning by chunking are not known.

As can be seen, the classical AI approach provides a perspective and capabilities that are substantially distinct from those of neurocomputation. Assessment of the ways in which these two approaches are complementary and mutually supportive is an important task for the future.

There are both pure and applied motivations for research on neurocomputation. It has a role in the much larger attempt to understand how mind is embodied in brain. In the present case the basic aim is to discover how knowledge is embodied in neocortex, and to clarify the functional consequences of that embodiment. Many possible applications of such work in education and medicine are discussed in the report of a large conference held in 1974 to survey research on the neural mechanisms of learning and memory (Rosenzweig & Bennett, 1976). The main change since then is that possible implications for the design of radically new adaptive computers have become the major practical motivation. At this early stage progress towards both pure and applied goals may be achieved by very much the same route.

4.1 Brief Historical Perspective

Formal mathematical attempts to show how basic cognitive capacities can arise from neural activity date back to at least the work of Pitts and McCulloch in the early 1940s (McCulloch, 1965). Formal mathematical studies of this kind seemed to Hebb (1949) to simplify the psychological problem nearly out of existence. He therefore built his account of the organisation of behaviour on a less formal account of neural activity and its modifiability, but one as faithful as possible to the neurobiological evidence then available. Computer simulation extended the range of techniques available for the theoretical study of adaptive neural nets, and the momentum gained during these years is reflected in Rosenblatt's (1962) ambitious book *Principles of Neurodynamics*.

Despite widespread study, however, the capabilities of such systems remained limited. In *perceptrons*, Minsky and Papert (1969) presented a formal analysis displaying the inherent limitations of the kind of nets being studied, and in particular their inability to learn anything other than linear combinations of their inputs, with the consequence that they cannot learn descriptions showing how different parts of the input related to each other. Minsky and Papert proposed instead the symbol processing approach that has formed the mainstream of artificial intelligence work since then. Cognitive science, therefore, arose during a period when enthusiasm for neural net approaches was declining, and it was based from the outset upon conceptions of information processing that did not include any consideration of the style of computation to which neural systems are suited.

Neurobiology was little affected by these developments within cognitive science, however, and studies of the neural basis of learning and memory continued to grow rapidly. Most of these were at the cellular level, and many were on simple invertebrate nervous systems or tissue culture preparations (e.g. Rosenzweig & Bennett, 1976). This work provided strong support for the idea that learning involves synaptic plasticity, and understanding of the mechanisms of this plasticity is now well advanced (e.g. Lynch, McGaugh, & Weinberger, 1984; Farley & Alkon, 1985).

The influence of neural net studies on cognitive psychology has until recently been minimal. Their importance and implications for cognitive theory were strongly emphasised by workers such as Grossberg (1982), however, and since the early 1980s (e.g. Hinton & Anderson, 1981) interest has been growing rapidly, particularly in the U.S.A. (e.g. Rumelhart & McClelland, 1986).

Physical systems and engineering research on neural nets is also currently growing rapidly. This is in part due to the work of Hopfield (1982), who showed how the dynamics of neural nets could be analysed by analogy with the dynamics of disordered magnetic spins. This analogy involves defining an energy function for the state of the net at any moment, and studying the conditions under which the energy of the net decreases. The central point of this work is to show how the memories of the net can be seen as energy minima, or attractor states, towards which the activity of the net converges, with the consequence that the net can rapidly retrieve the whole of a data-structure from arbitrary parts of it, and can even still do so when the part given contains errors. Content addressing with error correction has many uses but is difficult to achieve in conventional computers. Neural nets are therefore of considerable interest to designers of computers with a new range of capabilities (e.g. Eckmiller & von der Malsburg, 1988).

Study of the computational capabilities of neural nets is in its infancy. We therefore cannot present a long established and generally accepted position. Furthermore, the field is currently developing so rapidly that predictions of its future course must be highly speculative. The field as a whole is best seen as an interdisciplinary research area rather than as a theoretical position. We will first outline some of the major issues in the theoretical study of the computational capabilities of neural nets and then briefly discuss the relations between these studies and the relevant areas of cognitive psychology and neurobiology. Neural net research involves concepts that will not be familiar to many readers. For an extensive introduction, see Rumelhart & McClelland (1986), and for shorter and more simple introductions, see Johnson-Laird (1988) and Phillips (1988).

4.2 Computational Models of Neural Nets

This approach is essentially one of synthesis. Possible system designs are specified, and are then built or simulated so that their computational capabilities can be studied. Braitenberg (1985) illustrates the value of this strategy by his principle of downhill synthesis and uphill analysis which concerns methods for achieving understanding of systems in which complex behaviour results from simple underlying processes. He proposes that this will be more easily done by synthesising the behaviour from the processes than by analysing the behaviour into the processes from which it has arisen. This strategy clearly depends upon neurobiology and cognitive psychology, however, because they help specify the systems to synthesise and the capacities to investigate.

4.3 Major Design Issues

4.3.1 Connection Architecture.

This specifies how many units there are and how they are connected. A great variety of architectures have been studied. The simplest are auto-associative nets, in which there is just one layer of units with a high degree of interconnection within the layer, and hetero-associative nets, in which there are two layers with a high degree of connectivity from the first to the second layer. It was the inherent limitations of these kinds of nets that Minsky and Papert emphasised. Other architectures are therefore now receiving extensive attention. For example, multilayered feed-forward nets are an extension of hetero-associative nets to multiple layers. These can then include various patterns of connectivity within layers. Architectures with various forms of feedback connectivity are also under study. In choosing between the endless variety of possible architectures, the challenge is to discover a balance between innate structure and adaptability that enables effective performance within the task domain.

4.3.2 Representation.

Information in neural nets is represented by the activity of units within a defined population. In some systems each possible item is represented by the activity of a single unit, and in others by a pattern of activity defined across the population as a whole. Between complete localisation and complete distribution there is a range of semi-distributed representations in which items are represented by the activity of overlapping subsets of the population. Furthermore, when an item is represented by a set of units the individual units in that set may or may not represent the "micro-features" of which the item is composed. Other schemes are also possible. For example, the idea of using points in state space to represent items can be extended to the use of attractor regions in state space, the boundaries of which may be probabilistic and context sensitive. A better understanding of the strengths and weaknesses of different forms of representation and their implication for other aspects of system design is likely to emerge in the near future.

4.3.3 Learning.

The learning rules in adaptive neural net systems specify how the strengths of the connections between units change as a function of the activity of the units being connected, and also possibly as a function of other values computed at more distant sites in the net and made available locally. A wide variety of learning rules are being studied. They are often divided into those that are explicitly error correcting, and those that are not. The latter usually depend only upon the states of the two units being connected, and sometimes also upon the current strength of the connection between them. Well known examples are the original rule proposed by Hebb (1949), the linear associator, and competitive learning rules (Rumelhart & McClelland, 1986). Error correcting rules require a third signal specifying a desired or target state in addition to the two activity signals required by the former rules. The best known are the perceptron learning rule, and the closely related Widrow-Hoff and Delta rules. Specification of a version of the Delta rule that enables learning in multilayer nets is a major recent advance (e.g. Rumelhart, Hinton, & Williams, 1986).

4.3.4 Other Issues.

Other important design issues concern the functions specifying how the activity and output of the units are computed and updated. Important aspects of these decisions are whether the functions should be stochastic or deterministic, and whether the updating should be synchronous or asynchronous. Although linear activation and output functions are frequently used as approximations, there seems to be general agreement that non-linear functions are more realistic.

Major contributions to the task of showing how the collective computational properties of neural nets depend upon these various aspects of design are currently being made by workers in mathematics and the physical sciences, as well as by those in computing and cognitive science. Even at this stage, however, some general principles of computational significance are established.

4.4 Collective Computational Properties

4.4.1 Knowledge and Skill Acquisition by Learning.

In neural net systems the knowledge is in the connections, but the effect of any connection is highly dependent upon very many others. Explicitly programming such systems at the level of the connections is therefore prohibitively difficult. The ability of adaptive neural nets to acquire knowledge from experience by autonomous locally specified modifications to their connections is therefore essential to their viability.

4.4.2 Multiple Simultaneous Constraint Satisfaction.

A high degree of context sensitivity is a well-established feature of natural information processing. The use to be made of any part of the information available usually depends upon many other parts. Neural nets are able to balance multiple simultaneous constraints rapidly because of their high degree of interconnectivity (e.g. Tank & Hopfield, 1987). This enables them to achieve global states which although they may not be optimal are usually good approximations.

4.4.3 Content Addressing.

Fast error-correcting content addressing is a well-established property of neural net matrix memories (e.g. Kohonen, 1984) on which Hopfield (1982) has recently shed more light. It is of particular use when applying large knowledge structures to unpredictable problems. Intensive theoretical and technological investigations of the way that attractor states in neural nets provide this capability are being carried out in many laboratories in Europe and elsewhere (e.g. Bienenstock, Fogelman, & Weisbuch, 1986).

4.4.4 Abstraction, Generalisation and Interference.

Neural nets with distributed representations automatically abstract and generalise because the patterns of activation occurring at different times affect overlapping sets of connections (Rumelhart & McClelland, 1986). Common components of those patterns of activation therefore reinforce each other, and thereby discover the associative themes that run through the experience of the net. With the rich representation of experience in these nets the themes discovered may be at a refined level of analysis. As a result, complex rules relating different aspects of experience can be embodied in the connections. Furthermore, exceptions to the rules can be embodied in the same way without removing the ability of the net to use whatever regularity is present. Interaction between the records of different experiences is not guaranteed to be beneficial, however, and in some circumstances will produce effects better described as interference.

4.4.5 Fault Tolerance.

The knowledge embodied in these nets is usually widely distributed. Faulty function of their units, therefore, tends to have effects proportional to the extent of the malfunction. In addition, adaptive reorganisation after damage is a natural consequence of the modification of their connectivity as a function of experience.

4.5 Applications

A basic aim in the design of biological and technological nets that learn is that they be able to handle a wide variety of unpredictable tasks. Abstract specification of the classes of task solvable by different classes of neural net systems is a major research goal. Even at this early stage of development adaptive neural net models have been applied to a wide variety of tasks, including face recognition, letter recognition, phoneme recognition, speech processing, grapheme to phoneme conversion, and many others. For extensive discussions of the design and applications of neurocomputers, see Eckmiller and von der Malsburg (1988).

The range of applications to which these systems are uniquely well suited is wide because of their ability to acquire and rapidly apply large amounts of knowledge in noisy situations not governed by unbroken laws but by complex context-sensitive regularities with numerous exceptions. In our opinion finding uses for neural net computation is not going to be a problem. Technological developments are likely to be so extensive that in the short and medium term they could overshadow attempts to discover what specific neural net designs nature itself employs.

4.6 Unresolved Problems

Many issues concerning the way in which the elementary computational properties mentioned above depend upon architecture, representation, learning, and their integration remain to be resolved. For example, there is a need for learning algorithms that discover representations that are effective but are not specified by any supervisor, that minimise interference between records that should be kept distinct, and that learn quickly enough to be useful. Studies of the psychological and physiological plausibility of the back-propagation learning procedure (Rumelhart & McClelland, 1986) are also needed. The following indicates some other issues that also currently seem critical.

Much of the learning in neural net models to date has depended upon the investigator's choice of an appropriate representation of the information to be presented to the net, thereby neglecting the fundamental issue of how neural net systems can discover their own representations. Effective procedures of feature discovery to bridge the gap between sensory data and the more conceptual memory levels are therefore needed, and this is an area of substantial current activity. Similar basic problems concern the way in which the relations between the parts of an object, and between parts and wholes, are best represented in such systems.

The view that the serial symbol processing and adaptive net approaches are in opposition still continues to be common, but does not appear to be well founded. Few, if any, workers would claim that there is no level of description at which human thought has serial symbol processing characteristics, and few would claim that adaptive neurocomputers will make conventional computers obsolete. The challenge is not to choose between these two design philosophies, but to discover how they can be combined. Such a combination may help solve the problem of how words are related to the world. Part of the problem of relating the parallel and the serial levels of operation concerns the representation of sequence and, although this is still unresolved, important advances are being made. In general, there is much yet to discover about the temporal behaviour of these systems beyond that of the relaxation searches that find energy minima given static inputs.

Distribution of function within and between modular subsystems does not imply that there are no subsystems that specialise in high-level control and co-ordination. Furthermore, evidence from cognitive psychology and from neuropsychology indicates that central executive functions must be seriously considered. Some of the current theories of high-level voluntary control are in principle compatible with this approach (e.g. Norman & Shallice, 1980), but an adequate neurocomputational account of such functions is not available at present and will be a major focus of research during the next few years.

Most of the neurocomputational models studied to date are homogeneous in the sense that even when they have distinct levels or modules the essential design features are the same for all. In more complex and realistic systems different classes of modules are likely to have different computational requirements. A major research goal will be to determine how these requirements differ, and how the design features of the different components should be adapted to meet them.

4.7 Cognitive Psychology

Cognitive psychology has established many properties of learning and memory, some of wide generality, but is still seeking a coherent and generally agreed conceptual framework within which to describe and explain these phenomena. Neurocomputational approaches suggest a new starting point in the search for a shared conceptual framework. The capabilities that some of the most general phenomena require fit well with what neural nets provide. Simple examples are the ability to learn very many different items and the associations between them, to retrieve information rapidly on the basis of partial and noisy cues, to degrade gracefully, and to abstract concepts or schema from the regularities underlying varying input. Cognitive psychology already offers many other theories of each of these phenomena. In the area of concept and schema abstraction, for example, there is a variety of different formal and informal theories. The advantage of the neurocomputational approach is that it provides an explanation for a number of these general phenomena within a framework that is both computationally adequate and neurally plausible. What the study of learning and memory at the neural network level may therefore provide is a set of functional primitives into which more complex cognitive functions can be analysed. These functional primitives are explicitly derived from a study of the style of computation to which neural systems are suited. Explicit derivation is necessary because the functions such work proposes are computationally powerful, and from other perspectives would seem "like an appeal to magic".

It is important to note that the functional primitives of neurocomputational and conventional von Neumann computing systems are quite different. Attempts to explain the performance of one in terms of the functional primitives of the other are therefore likely to run into difficulty. It is possible that the conceptions of "information processing" on which cognitive theory has been based have either been too general to provide an effective starting point, or have been inappropriately derived from analogies with von Neumann computing. For example, one consequence of the knowledge being in the connections is that it *directly* determines processing. Memory and processing are therefore not distinguished in the way that they are in von Neumann computation.

Another consequence of this approach is that it could help unite the cognitive and S–R associative learning traditions. Although the attempt to explain higher cognitive functions on the basis of associative learning principles (e.g. Skinner's account of verbal behaviour) was not convincing, the basic properties of associative learning, such as first- and second-order conditioning, compound conditioning, Kamin blocking, and extinction, are ubiquitous. Indeed, they vary so little across the phylogenetic scale that it is possible to defend the thesis that they do not vary at all. It is, therefore, significant that the connection modification rule most used in neural net memories is equivalent to the Rescorla-Wagner rule that summarises much of the associative learning literature (Sutton & Barto, 1981). In the PDP approach it is called the Delta rule and was that used in Rumelhart and McClelland's simulation of past tense learning. The neurocomputational approach, therefore, may also contribute to the study of cognitive evolution.

We have been arguing that neurocomputational approaches may contribute to the development of theory in cognitive psychology, but cognitive psychology also has much to contribute to neurocomputational research. This is already clear in that some of the well-established properties of cognition seem to call for such explanations. For example, the high degree of context sensitivity demonstrated by such phenomena as the word and object superiority effects, led McClelland and Rumelhart to propose the interactive activation model. Although this model was not initially motivated by neurocomputational design considerations it was clearly highly compatible with them. Much of the subsequent work on PDP systems has been clearly activated by the findings and theories of cognitive psychology (Rumelhart & McClelland, 1986). The major design issues in neurocomputational modelling, such as architecture, representation, and learning all relate to major topics in cognitive psychology, cognitive neuropsychology, and the study of associative learning. The relevance of experimental cognitive psychology to neurocomputational research is well illustrated by Schneider and Detweller's (1987) development of a neural net system based on the working memory research of Baddeley and Hitch and others. Many other combined computational and experimental investigations are now under way (e.g. Gluck & Bower, 1988) The value of this contribution will be more dependent on the extent to which it helps choose between alternative neurocomputational designs than on the extent to which it supports the neurocomputational approach in comparison to other approaches. The explicit design of new experimental paradigms to meet this requirement is, therefore, a major challenge to and opportunity for cognitive psychology.

4.8 Neurobiology

Rumelhart and McClelland list the following as fundamental neurobiological constraints on cognitive theories: neurons are slow; there is a very large number of neurons; neurons receive inputs from a large number of other neurons; learning involves modifying connections; neurons communicate by sending activation or inhibition through connections; connections in the brain seem to have a clear geometric and topological structure; information is continuously available; graceful degradation with damage and information overload; distributed, not central, control; relaxation is the dominant mode of computation. Although details of their argument are debatable, the neural net models that are used to simulate cognitive performance are clearly based upon neurobiological foundations. It is therefore appropriate to briefly outline some major features of the relation between neurobiology and neurocomputational modelling.

Beyond the elementary constraints such as those listed, neurocomputational studies vary greatly in the extent to which they incorporate further neurobiological information. At one extreme they make no further use of neuroscience, while at the other they incorporate as much further information as possible. The aim of the former sort is usually to study the capabilities and limitations of neural nets in general. However, those studies that aim to contribute to our understanding of human cognition are concerned with a particular neural net system and will benefit from a greater input from neurobiology, and from knowledge of human or primate neocortical organisation in particular.

It is therefore likely that future neurocomputational models of human cognition will incorporate more information on the variety of cellular structures, and on cortical circuitry. Peter Sandon, of the Computer Science Department, University of Wisconsin, says "Designing connectionist networks at the processing element level is like designing operating systems at the gate level." Knowledge of the patterns of connectivity within and between cortical columns and between cortical regions will provide a vital source of information for designing circuits that are intermediate between the unit and the module. A crucial issue in this context is whether there is a general pattern of cortical connectivity that is repeated in many different cortical regions. There are variations in anatomy across the neocortex and, on the basis of these differences, Brodmann identified about 50 different areas per human hemisphere. The differences are so subtle, however, that they are frequently disputed by anatomists. Even across different species gross cortical structure remains remarkably constant. The area and thickness varies but the basic structure does not. The columnar and hyper-columnar organisation, first found in somatic and primary visual areas, appears to be repeated in all or most other cortical areas (Mountcastle, 1978). The neuroanatomists, Rockel, Hiorns, and Powell (1980), in an article entitled "The basic uniformity in structure of the neo-cortex", say:

> The significance of the columnar organization is in the processing of incoming
> information, vertically within a column, and horizontally between columns, with a wide

and diverse distribution of the results through the pyramidal cell axons; the form of the processing might be essentially similar in all areas but the differences in function between areas would be due to the differences in the sources and termination of their connections.

If this hypothesis is correct, then it gives this work a clear and fundamental goal: to specify precisely what this design is, what its computational capabilities are, and how those capabilities enable knowledge to be so effectively embodied in the neocortex.

There is a great deal of evidence on the cellular and biochemical basis of synaptic plasticity, but more information on plasticity at the neural network level is needed. For example, we need to know how plastic and fixed connections are combined within the circuit design, what constraints there are on increases and decreases in synaptic efficiency, how plasticity is distributed across excitatory and inhibitory synapses, what conditions determine whether synaptic modification should occur, and what effect feedback from later processing stages has on learning in earlier stages. More information is also needed on the rules that specify synaptic modification; are they close to that originally proposed by Hebb, error correcting as in the Delta rule, or of some other form? It is also important to discover whether one rule applies to the cortex as a whole, or whether different versions apply to regions with different computational roles. The role of theory in guiding the experimental investigation of plasticity is well illustrated by the case of fast temporary changes in synaptic connectivity. The possibility that such changes could be combined with the longer-lasting modifications was suggested by von der Malsburg (1986) on theoretical grounds, and Hinton has suggested that they could function to adapt new learning to old. Experimental investigations now under way are beginning to provide physiological evidence for such a process.

Finally, the recent computational models provide neurobiology with a new perspective on representation. Although it has long been clear that local single-unit grand-mother cell encoding was only one possibility, and in many ways an implausible one, population cooperative encoding theories were not well enough specified to provide a testable alternative. Precise specification of cooperative encodings are now possible, and their predictions concerning how single units should behave if part of such a cooperative can be tested.

4.9 Interdisciplinary Cooperation

Neurocomputational models try to bridge the gap between neural activity and mental function. Furthermore, their concern with the collective behaviour of highly interactive dynamical systems draws upon the analyses developed by mathematicians and physicists for analogous systems, and their implications for computer design makes them highly relevant to engineers and computer scientists. The approach is therefore highly interdisciplinary, and a variety of active collaborations already exist. Such variety should be encouraged.

Neurobiological and cognitive studies of learning and memory have until now been for the most part independent. This independence even extends to the recently flourishing area known as cognitive neuropsychology, which despite its title involves little or no formal consideration of the neural basis of cognition, and might be more accurately entitled clinical cognitive psychology. The reason for this independence is that there has been no adequate theory linking the two disciplines. The neurocomputational approach may provide such a linking theory.

To illustrate the scope for interdisciplinary cooperation, just three of many possible large-scale projects will be briefly outlined. These focus on object recognition, functional specialisation in reading, and the search for a general purpose cortical architecture and learning algorithm. The study of our knowledge of objects, its acquisition, and use in perception, could combine experimental studies of normal and agnosic subjects, neurophysiological and anatomical studies of implicated cortical and subcortical regions, and neurocomputational modelling of these functions. Cognitive studies of functional specialisation in reading in both normal and dyslexic subjects are now well advanced. Neurocomputational modelling of some of these functions has already begun, but a single model combining all the major components has not yet been attempted. It is probably feasible at this stage to produce such a model, and to combine it with the work on a connectionist control architecture for working memory. A major goal of such a program could be to provide a system of distinct but interacting modules that illustrates aspects of overall system design and functional specialisation. Such a program would require major contributions from cognitive psychologists, neuropsychologists, and linguists, in addition to neural modellers and very substantial computing power. Finally, the possibility of a general purpose "cortical algorithm" at the centre of learning and memory should not be neglected. The search for such an algorithm could combine attempts to discover general principles of cortical connectivity and plasticity with simulation studies of learning, abstraction, and interference.

5. THE EUROPEAN CONTEXT AND POSSIBLE FORMS OF SUPPORT

Europe has been a world leader in the scientific study of learning and memory since the beginning of experimental psychology 100 years ago up to and including the cognitive psychology of the last 20 years. It has a particular pre-eminence in the emerging field of cognitive neuropsychology, which builds upon the long traditions of clinical neurology and clinical neuropsychology in Europe. These strengths must be capitalised upon to build a broadly based but coherent understanding of learning and memory that will be a crucial part of both basic science and technology.

There is also a strong tradition of research on the neurobiology of learning and memory, including both experimental and theoretical approaches. There is at present not such a pre-eminence in connectionist approaches to computing, nor in the parallel distributed processing approaches to cognition. Work in these areas is currently centred in the U.S.A. The importance of support for neurocomputational research has already been recognised in Europe, however. For example, the Science Stimulation Fund of Directorate-General XII, of the European Commission, has created the initiative BRAIN (Basic Research in Adaptive Intelligence and Neurocomputing), the West German government is setting up an Institute specialising in this field, and a North Atlantic Advanced Research Workshop was held in Dusseldorf in September, 1987, on "Neural Computers: From Computational Neuroscience to Computer Design" (reported in Eckmiller & von der Malsburg, 1988). These and other initiatives show that there is a promising future for this area in Europe. However, in all of the initiatives mentioned there is a clear need for a greater involvement of cognitive psychology.

Research funding at the national level is clearly inadequate to meet the great challenges and opportunities presented by the state of basic research on learning and memory. European level support is essential. Substantial resources are available, and their effective use will undoubtedly involve a variety of procedures. One possibility is to identify key areas to be given particular support. The success of such a procedure depends crucially upon the specification of the key areas, and there should be a clear investment in this stage, with the aim of finding areas that are smaller and more precisely specified than in other such initiatives. One way such a specification might be made is by calling European level meetings to discuss possible areas. These should involve experts from as wide a range of relevant disciplines as possible, with support being given only where a clear, coherent, and widely agreed case emerges. Applications for research contracts in the targeted area could then be called for and allocated much as usual. However, we would encourage increased flexibility in the conditions attached to the contracts. For example, Science Stimulation contracts specify that all research workers employed on the contract be nationals of an EEC country. While this may be a useful guideline to be met where possible, it is too restrictive in its present form. It is more important that this work be done in Europe than that it be done solely by Europeans. The research programmes would also be strengthened by provision for contractors meetings, to which contractors could invite experts in related fields to survey progress in the designated area. Such a procedure is used by the Sloan Foundation and the Department of Defense in the U.S.A. and works well.

Many of the areas discussed above are highly interdisciplinary. Provision for a variety of cross-disciplinary training procedures is therefore vital. This could take such forms as travelling fellowships, summer schools, and support for postgraduate training courses that are specifically designed to bridge related disciplines.

Finally, research in some areas of learning and memory could be enhanced by greater availability of appropriate computing resources. There is a growing agreement that greater access to transputer arrays, or hardware specifically designed for massively parallel neuronal computing, will substantially enhance neurocomputational research over the next decade or so. A similar conclusion is also proposed in relation to the work on vision. The community should therefore specifically foster the development of these systems and the appropriate software support, and make them as widely available as possible.

ACKNOWLEDGEMENTS

We are grateful to our colleagues in the FAST cognitive psychology section for comments on an earlier draft and to Richard Young for providing the section on machine learning.

REFERENCES

Anderson, J.R. (1986). Knowledge compilation: The general learning mechanism. In R.S. Michalski, J.G. Carbonell, & T.M. Mitchell (Eds), *Machine learning: An artificial intelligence approach*, Vol. 2. Palo Alto, Calif.: Morgan Kaufmann.

Anderson, J.R. (1987). Skill acquisition: Compilation of weak-method problem solutions. *Psychological Review, 94*, 192-210.

Atkinson, R.C. & Shiffrin, R.M. (1968). Human memory: A proposed system and its control processes. In K.W. Spence (Ed.), *The psychology of learning and motivation: Advances in research and theory*, Vol. 2, pp. 89-195. London and San Diego: Academic Press.

Baddeley, A.D. (1966a). Short-term memory for word sequences as a function of acoustic, semantic and formal similarity. *Quarterly Journal of Experimental Psychology, 18*, 362-365.

Baddeley, A.D. (1966b). The influence of acoustic and semantic similarity on long-term memory for word sequences. *Quarterly Journal of Experimental Psychology, 18*, 302-309.

Baddeley, A.D. (1986). *Working memory*. Oxford: Oxford University Press.

Baddeley, A.D. (in press). *Human Memory: Theory and Practice*. London: Lawrence Erlbaum Associates Ltd.

Baddeley, A.D. & Hitch, G.J. (1974). Working memory. In G. Bower (Ed.), *Recent advances in learning and motivation*, Vol. VIII, pp. 47-90. London and San Diego: Academic Press.

Bienenstock, E., Fogelman, F., & Weisbuch, G. (Eds) (1986). *Disordered systems and biological organization*. Berlin: Springer-Verlag.

Braitenberg, B. (1985). *Vehicles: Experiments in synthetic psychology*. Cambridge, Mass.: MIT Press.

Bundy, A., Silver, B., & Plummer, D. (1985). An analytical comparison of some rule-learning programs. *Artificial Intelligence, 27*, 137-181.

Collins, A.M. & Loftus, E.F. (1975). A spreading-activation theory of semantic processing. *Psychological Review, 82*, 407-428.

Conrad, C. (1972). Cognitive economy in semantic memory. *Journal of Experimental Psychology, 92*, 149-154.

Craik, F.I.M. & Lockhart, R.S. (1972). Levels of processing: A framework for memory research. *Journal of Verbal Learning and Verbal Behavior, 11*, 671-684.

Crowder, R.G. (1976). *Principles of learning and memory*. Hillsdale, N.J.: Lawrence Erlbaum Associates Inc.

Eckmiller, R. & von der Malsburg, C. (1988). *Neural computers*. NATO ASI Series, Series F, Vol. 41. Berlin: Springer-Verlag.

Farley, J. & Alkon, D.L. (1985). Cellular mechanisms of learning, memory, and information storage. *Annual Review of Psychology, 36*, 419-494.

Glanzer, M. & Cunitz, A.R. (1966). Two storage mechanisms in free recall. *Journal of Verbal Learning and Verbal Behavior, 5*, 351-360.

Gluck, M.A. & Bower, G.H. (1988). Evaluating an adaptive network model of human learning. *Journal of Memory and Language, 27*, 166-195.

Grossberg, S. (1982). *Studies of mind and brain*. Boston: Reidel Press.

Hebb, D.O. (1949). *The organization of behavior*. New York: John Wiley.

Hinton, G.E. & Anderson, J.A. (Eds) (1981). *Parallel models of associative memory*. Hillsdale, N.J.: Lawrence Erlbaum Associates Inc.

Hopfield, J.J. (1982). Neural networks and physical systems with emergent collective computational abilities. *Proceedings of the National Academy of Sciences, USA, 79*, 2554-2558.

Johnson-Laird, P.N. (1988). *The Computer and the Mind*. London: Fontana.

Kintsch, W. (1980). Semantic memory: A tutorial. In R. Nickerson (Ed.), *Attention and performance VIII*, pp.595-620. Hillsdale, N.J.: Lawrence Erlbaum Associates Inc.

Kintsch, W. & van Dijk, T.A. (1978). Toward a model of text comprehension and production. *Psychological Review, 85*, 363-394.

Kohonen, T. (1984). *Self-organization and associative memory*. Berlin: Springer-Verlag.

Kopelman, M.D. (1986). The cholinergic neurotransmitter system in human memory and dementia: A review. *Quarterly Journal of Experimental Psychology, 38A*, 535-574.

Laird, J.E., Rosenbloom, P.S., & Newell, A. (1986a). Chunking in Soar: The anatomy of a general learning mechanism. *Machine Learning, 1*, 11-46.

Laird, J.E., Rosenbloom, P.S., & Newell, A. (1986b). *Universal subgoaling and chunking: The automatic generation and learning of goal hierarchies*. Hingham, MA.: Kluwer.

Laird, J.E., Newell, A., & Rosenbloom, P.S. (1987). SOAR: An architecture for general intelligence. *Artificial Intelligence, 33*, 1-64.

Lynch, G., McGaugh, J.L., & Weinberger, N.M. (Eds) (1984). *Neurobiology of learning and memory*. New York: Guilford Press.

McCulloch, W.S. (1965). *Embodiments of mind*. Cambridge, Mass.: MIT. Press.

von der Malsburg, C. (1986). Am I thinking assemblies? In G. Palm & A. Aertsen (Eds), *Brain theory*, pp.161-176. Berlin: Springer-Verlag.

Michalski, R.S., Carbonell, J.G., & Mitchell, T.M. (Eds) (1983). *Machine learning: An artificial intelligence approach*, Vol. 1. Palo Alto, Calif.: Tioga Publishing.

Michalski, R.S., Carbonell, J.G., & Mitchell, T.M. (Eds) (1986). *Machine learning: An artificial intelligence approach*, Vol. 2. Palo Alto, Calif.: Morgan Kaufmann.

Milner, B. (1966). Amnesia following operation on the temporal lobes. In C.W.M. Whitty & O.L. Zangwill (Eds), *Amnesia*, pp. 109-133. London: Butterworths.

Minsky, M. & Papert, S. (1969). *Perceptrons*. Cambridge, Mass.: MIT. Press.

Mishkin, M. (1982). A memory system in the monkey. *Philosophical Transactions of the Royal Society London, B298*, 85-95.

Mountcastle, V.B. (1978). An organizing principle for central function: The unit module and the distributed system. In G.M. Edelman & V.B. Mountcastle (Eds), *The mindful brain*. Cambridge, Mass.: MIT. Press.

Neisser, U. (1978). Memory: What are the important questions? In M.M. Gruneberg, P.E. Morris, & R.N. Sykes (Eds), *Practical aspects of memory*. London and San Diego: Academic Press.

Newell, A. (in preparation). *Unified theories of cognition: The 1987 William James Lectures*.

Nilsson, L.G. & Archer, T. (1985). *Perspectives on memory research*. Hillsdale, N.J.: Lawrence Erlbaum Associates Inc.

Norman, D.A. & Shallice, T. (1980). Attention to action. Willed and automatic control of behavior. *University of California San Diego CHIP Report 99*.

Phillips, W.A. (1988). Brainy minds. *Quarterly Journal of Experimental Psychology, 40A(2)*, 389-405.

Quillian, M.R. (1969). The teachable language comprehender: A simulation program and theory of language. *Communications of the Association for Computing Machinery, 12*, 459-476.

Rockel, A.J., Hiorns, R.W., & Powell, T.P.S. (1980). The basic uniformity in structure of the neocortex. *Brain, 103*, 221-244.

Rosenblatt, F. (1962). *Principles of neurodynamics*. New York: Spartan.

Rosenbloom, P.S. & Newell, A. (1986). The chunking of goal hierarchies: A generalized model of practice. In R.S. Michalski, J.G. Carbonell & T.M. Mitchell (Eds), *Machine learning: An artificial intelligence approach*, Vol. 2. Palo Alto, Calif.: Morgan Kaufmann.

Rosenzweig, M.R. & Bennett, E.L. (Eds) (1976). *Neural mechanisms of learning and memory*. Cambridge, Mass.: MIT. Press.

Rumelhart, D.E. & McClelland, J.L. (Eds) (1986). *Parallel distributed processing*, Vols 1 and 2. Cambridge, Mass.: MIT. Press.

Rumelhart, D.E., Hinton, G.E., & Williams, R.J. (1986). Learning representations by back-propagating errors. *Nature*, *323*, 533-536.

Schank, R.C. (1982). *Dynamic memory*. New York: Cambridge University Press.

Schneider, W. & Detweller, M. (1987). A connectionist/control architecture for working memory. In G.H. Bower (Ed.), *The psychology of learning and motivation*, Vol. 21. London and San Diego: Academic Press.

Shallice, T. & Warrington, E.K. (1970). Independent functioning of the verbal memory stores: A neuropsychological study. *Quarterly Journal of Experimental Psychology*, *22*, 261-273.

Silver, B. (1986). Precondition analysis: learning control information. In R.S. Michalski, J.G. Carbonell & T.M. Mitchell (Eds), *Machine learning: An artificial intelligence approach*, Vol. 2. Palo Alto, Calif.: Morgan Kaufmann.

Squire, L. (1982). The neuropsychology of human memory. *Annual Review of Neuroscience*, *5*, 241-273.

Sutton, R.S. & Barto, A.G. (1981). Toward a modern theory of adaptive networks: Expectation and prediction. *Psychological Review*, *88*, 135-170.

Tank, D.W. & Hopfield, J.J. (1987). Collective computation in neuronlike circuits. *Scientific American*, *257*, 62-70.

Tulving, E. (1984). Multiple review of elements of episodic memory. *Behavioral and Brain Sciences*.

Valler, G. (In press). Neuropsychology. In M. Imbert & N.O. Bernsen (Eds). *Research directions in cognitive science: A European perspective, Volume . Neurobiology*. London: Lawrence Erlbaum Associates Ltd.

Wilson, G.T., Franks, C.M., Brownell, K.D., & Kendal, P.C. (1984). *Annual review of behaviour therapy: Theory and practice*, Vol. 9. New York: Guilford Press.

CHAPTER 5

Problem Solving, Reasoning and Decision Making

Jonathan St. B. T. Evans

Plymouth Polytechnic, Drakes Circus,
Plymouth PL4 8AA, England

INTRODUCTION

The topics of thinking and reasoning have perhaps the longest history of psychological study among the subject matter of modern cognitive psychology, dating back at least to the writings of Aristotle. The area has been consistently researched since the evolution of psychology as a distinct scientific discipline in the mid nineteenth century and is incorporated within the contemporary discipline of cognitive psychology as the study of "higher" cognitive processes.

The psychology of human thought should be regarded as quite central to the problems of cognitive science. The perception of patterns and objects, the decoding of language, the retrieval of memories and the representation of knowledge are all vital constituents of intelligent activity. However, the resultant representations are almost always subject to further mental processes whose purpose is to draw inferences, solve problems, generate judgements and forecasts, or to decide between alternative courses of action. Ultimate cognitive acts whose nature reflects the purpose of the intelligent system, be it human or artificial, inevitably involve the operation of such higher cognitive processes.

In the context of the FAST initiative this chapter should ideally summarise the history and current state of knowledge in the psychology of thinking, and then indicate fairly and clearly the range of issues which need to be explored in future research. In fact, I can only hope partially to achieve these aims due to two basic and insurmountable problems. The first is that a vast area of research activity and accumulated knowledge is involved to which justice simply cannot be done in the space available. The second is that no one individual (certainly not this author) can claim detailed expertise across such a range of topics. Inevitably, then, the coverage is to an extent both selective and reflective of my personal views of the salient issues.

In an attempt to counter these problems, I shall first of all indicate the major topics that are omitted. The whole area of cognitive development is not covered, despite the strong European tradition in the work of the Piagetian school, British psychologists such as Margaret Donaldson and many others. There should be no inference that developmental issues are unimportant (it was simply beyond the scope of this chapter and the competence of its author to provide such coverage). Of the adult literatures on the psychology of thought there is, in particular, no coverage of conceptual thinking, creativity or psychometric approaches to intelligence, nor of studies of non-directed thinking such as day-dreaming.

In order to make the task relatively manageable, I have concentrated on studies of directed thinking motivated by the achievement of goals. Kahney (1986) offers a simple but effective definition of problem solving, "A person has a 'problem' when he or she has a goal which cannot be achieved directly". This definition, however, does not simply apply to those tasks traditionally reported under the heading of "problem solving" but applies equally to those normally described as "reasoning" or "decision making". The requirement, for example, to check the logical validity of an argument is a problem with a clearly defined goal for which the subject must find an appropriate method of solution. Similarly, every decision to be made is effectively a problem to be solved. I have assumed that despite the different traditions and largely disjoint literatures associated with the three main topic areas discussed in this chapter, the underlying mental processes are essentially similar. For this reason, historical coverage of each topic is followed by an attempt to identify the common issues arising for future research. The histories are of necessity both brief and selective, so I have tried where possible to provide references to books or other secondary sources to which the reader can turn for a more detailed introduction to these topics.

Finally, whilst I have included reference to a number of significant European contributions to the topics discussed, this chapter is not intended to be a review of European research as such. I considered this to be an impractical objective in view of the international nature of the literatures which include major input from American researchers and those in other parts of the world. I also considered this to be an undesirable objective, since the purpose of the exercise is to look forward to future research, an effort which must surely be informed by an appraisal of the current state of knowledge regardless of its geographical origins.

HISTORICAL REVIEW

1 Problem Solving

By Kahney's definition, given above, problem solving refers to a very wide range of activity. Any of the following individuals may be described as having a problem which requires solving: a hungry person who must find something to eat, a student who wishes to pass an examination, someone late for an appointment and whose car refuses to start, a business manager forced to choose which staff to make redundant and so on and so on. Not surprisingly psychologists have wished to identify some general characteristics and processes to describe the almost unlimited range of activities denoted by the term "problem solving".

One useful definition is between well and ill defined problems. In a well defined problem, the problem solver has clear knowledge of the goals, constraints and methods available. Many of the problems studied by psychologists (and modelled in artificial intelligence (AI)) have been of this type. These problems are usually of a kind where an initial state can be changed into a goal state by a series of transformations (for general coverage of research on such problems see Kahney, 1986; Gilhooly, 1982; Mayer, 1983). For example, the Tower of Hanoi problem is one in which the subject must move a set of discs of different sizes from one peg to another via a third. The restriction is that the disc must always be placed only on top of other discs which are larger in size. The "states" of the system (initial, goal and intermediate) are defined by the current locations of the discs. This problem is so well defined that a simple algorithm can be described for its solution (for a variable number of discs) and implemented as a computer program.

Other problems are well defined in principle, but much less amenable to simple algorithmic solutions due to the sheer number of alternative possibilities to be considered (a good example is that of complex board games such as Chess and Go). Many real life problems, however, are ill-defined in that either the goals or the means available for solution are not clearly laid out at the start. The activity associated with such tasks thus involves defining the problem and its goal, and discovering possible means, as well as the application of methods of solution. Recently, psychologists have started to pay more attention to such ill-defined problems as in the work on analogical problem solving discussed later.

Historically, two particular periods of work stand out in the psychology of problem solving. The first is that of the pre-war Gestalt psychology school which stood against the prevailing philosophy of Watson's behaviourism (see Mandler & Mandler, 1964, for a detailed historical treatment of the rival schools). Approaching thinking from a wholist, field theoretic study of perception, Gestalt psychologists were wont to emphasise the importance of "insight" and "productive thinking" (cf. Wertheimer, 1961). A classic example is the nine dot problem in which the subject is asked to draw a line through each dot in a three by three grid pattern, using only four lines and without lifting the pen from the paper. Most subjects find this very difficult until it is pointed out that the lines may be drawn outside the boundary of the grid. The difficulty of the problem arises because the subject has imposed a constraint which was not in the wording of the problem, and which makes its solution impossible. Solution follows insight or "productive reformulation" in which the problem is perceived in a new way. In modern terms we would say that the difficulty of such a problem reflected errors in the mental representation of its essential characteristics.

Much of the Gestalt work was in fact concerned with factors which inhibited productive thinking. For example, the phenomena of "set" (Luchins, 1942) and "functional fixity" (Duncker, 1945) referred respectively to rigid adherence to patterns of thinking which had been reinforced by past success, and to the failure to consider the use of objects in problem solving for purposes other than that of their usual function. The origins of contemporary information processing approaches to problem solving can also be seen in the Gestalt studies as in the distinction between errors of representation and process, in the need to break problems down into subgoals and the development of "think aloud" protocols as a method of tracing thought processes (see particularly, Duncker, 1945); although of course they did not use this terminology.

The second major contribution which heavily influenced both psychological and AI approaches to problem solving was the work of Alan Newell and Herb Simon especially during the 1960s (see Newell and Simon, 1972, for an overview). Their theory of human problem solving was based firmly on the information processing model, and their work includes some of the earliest examples of psychological theories being expressed as working computer programs. This theory was based upon the state space representation applicable to well defined transformation problems, discussed earlier. Hence, problem solving was conceptualised as a search through a "problem space" consisting of an initial state, one or more goal stages and any number of intermediate states reachable by the application of legal "operators". In a chess game, for example, the states would be the board positions and the operators the laws of chess concerning legal game moves. Their most famous program was known as GPS (General Problem Solver) and was based on a central heuristic strategy known as "means-ends analysis".

Newell and Simon compared the performance of their programs to protocols obtained from human subjects by asking them to "think aloud" (a controversial technique which leads to an important methodological issue concerning the ability of people to verbalise their thoughts). This problem will be considered later. Leaving this issue aside (and despite the importance of their work) a number of criticisms can be offered in hindsight. For example, nearly all the problems they studied were of the well-defined type (usually transformation problems) to which their model was most easily applicable. Also, programs like GPS which were claimed to have very general problem solving abilities were in fact presented with highly abstract symbolic representations on which to work. In other words many of the vital aspects of the problem solving process involving perception, structuring and encoding of the essential characteristics of the problem domain were carried out by humans on behalf of the program.

The issue of verbalisation of thinking has been subject to major debate in recent literatures on both cognitive and social psychology. For example, Nisbett & Wilson (1977) argued strongly that people have no access to their own mental processes for the purpose of verbal report and construct their "introspections" on the basis of *a priori* causal theories. The evidence for this claim was based largely on evidence that subjects are unaware of the stimuli which cause changes in attitudes and social judgements, or even that changes have occurred at all. However, numerous subsequent papers in the social literature have challenged their arguments and evidence (see White, 1988, for a review).

Ericsson & Simon (1980; 1984) have also defended verbal protocol analysis as a method of "process tracing" in problem solving and decision making. They argue that such methods are not subject to the same problems as introspective reports because:

1. The verbalisations are concurrent rather than retrospective and hence a more accurate record of the current focus of the subjects' attention.

2. The method treats verbalisations as products of underlying cognitive processes to be interpreted by the experimenter and not as self-descriptions of strategies.

Nevertheless, Ericsson & Simon (1984) concede that such reports may be incomplete records for preconscious "recognition" processes or for those which have become "automatic" through overlearning. Recent experimental evidence of implicit processes in the learning of complex rules and control strategies suggest that they may have underestimated this incompleteness problem (see, for example, Reber et al 1980; Berry & Broadbent, 1984; Broadbent et al, 1986).

Another controversial issue arising from the Newell and Simon work lies in their assumption that problem solving largely reflects the operation of "weak methods" which are independent of domain knowledge. A number of recent studies have attributed much more significance to the use of knowledge in problem solving, by virtue of using more realistic, and less well defined problems. For example, there has been considerable interest in analogical problem solving in which subjects must seek the solution from prior knowledge gained outside of the problem solving situation (see, for example, Gick & Holyoak, 1980; 1983; Keane, 1988). An important theoretical notion here is that of the "schema" (a domain sensitive knowledge structure which includes *procedural knowledge* in the form of rules and methods which are applicable to problems of a given structure). The schema concept has a long history in psychology and an excellent discussion of its applicability to the psychology of thinking can be found in Rumelhart (1980).

2 Deductive Reasoning

Reasoning is a fundamental aspect of intelligent thought since it is the process by which different pieces of information are brought together in order to infer knowledge which is not directly known to the system. Most AI programs involve some form of reasoning (e.g. the inference engines of expert systems) and the language PROLOG is actually based directly upon first order predicate logic. Deductive reasoning refers to the drawing of inferences by use of logic in which the conclusions should be true provided that the premises upon which they are based are sound. Inductive and probabilistic inferences may also be important in cognitive science as many real world problems involve handling uncertainty (see part 3).

Deductive reasoning tasks administered by psychologists are usually modelled on one or another type of formal logic (e.g. classical syllogistic logic or the propositional calculus). Typically, a subject will be presented with the premises of an argument together with a possible conclusion and asked whether the conclusion follows logically from the argument. For example, Evans, Barston & Pollard (1983) gave subjects arguments in the form of classical, Aristotelian syllogisms such as the following:

No addictive things are inexpensive,
Some cigarettes are inexpensive,

Therefore, some addictive things are not cigarettes.

Instructions in a deductive reasoning task tend to emphasise the logical requirement that conclusions should be *necessarily* true given their premises. Hence, the subjects of Evans et al were asked to decide the truth of the conclusion "on the assumption that all the information given is, in fact, true. If you judge that a conclusion necessarily follows from the statements then you should answer 'yes', otherwise 'no'." Alternative methods involve giving subjects a choice of conclusions or asking them to draw their own. Other tasks in the deductive reasoning literature are more loosely constructed as hypothesis testing or decision making tasks involving understanding of logical relationships (see Evans, 1982, for detailed discussion).

Generally speaking, deductive reasoning tasks can be viewed as well defined problems, except that the means of solution (e.g. the laws of logic) is not provided. Discovering the mechanisms by which people reason (as well as their process of application) is a prime objective of such research. The general findings of such studies are that:

1. Subjects' responses frequently deviate from the logically defined solution.
2. Reasoning is highly sensitive to the (logically irrelevant) nature of the problem content and the context in which it is presented (see Evans, 1982; 1989, for relevant literature reviews).

Research on content effects involves holding the logical structure of problems constant whilst changing the meaning of the constituent propositions. Evidence has been accumulated to the effect that the knowledge invoked by meaningful content can have both biasing and debiasing effects. For example, there is a widespread, but oversimplified, belief that using concrete, realistic materials rather than abstract, artificial ones, facilitates logical performance (see Wason & Johnson-Laird, 1972). More recent research has shown that such facilitation in fact depends upon the subject having knowledge that is either directly relevant to the problem set, or which can be utilised by analogical reasoning (see Griggs, 1983). The biasing effects of knowledge occur when subjects' judgements of the validity of the conclusions of arguments are affected by their prior believability. For example, the problem shown above is one used by Evans et al (1983) in their investigation of this belief bias effect. This syllogism is logically invalid, but the conclusion is believable. Far more subjects endorsed the validity of this argument than an equivalent one with an unbelievable conclusion.

Until quite recently, the psychology of deductive reasoning was regarded by some as a rather isolated and insular field which made little contact with either the problem solving literature or main stream cognitive psychology in general. The reason for this lies not in any intrinsic irrelevance of the topic (far from it) but rather in a tendency for work to be focused too narrowly on the issue of logicality. A strong tradition, influenced by Piaget in Europe (e.g. Inhelder & Piaget, 1958) and by Mary Henle (e.g. 1962) in the USA, held that logic was the fundamental basis of human reasoning. The numerous demonstrations of illogical behaviour in psychological experiments have consequently been seen by some as an affront to be explained away by various devices. For example, it might be argued that :

1. Subjects reason logically from a personalised representation of problem information which differs from that intended by the experimenter.
2. Subjects use a different form of logic from the normative theory adopted by the experimenter.
3. Subjects are baffled by the artificial content of laboratory problems which inhibits demonstration of their real world competence.

All of the above types of arguments have been proposed quite recently by Cohen (1981) in a controversial attack on claims of errors and biases arising in the literatures on both deductive and probabilistic inference (see also part 3). However, despite the perseveration of the "rationality" debate, I would not wish to identify this as a key issue for future investigation. Much more interesting are the arguments arising within the past decade or so about the mechanisms which are responsible for reasoning; regardless of their conformity to logical norms. It is this recent work which has established reasoning research in its proper place within main stream cognitive psychology.

Recent authors (see Evans, 1989) have identified a number of alternative theoretical explanations for deductive reasoning based upon:

1. Inference rules.
2. Heuristics.
3. Schemas.
4. Mental models.

Most theorists consider that behaviour reflects both a competence and performance component. Competence refers to the underlying understanding (implicit or explicit) of logical principles or strategies that provides the potential to reason, whereas performance factors (e.g. working memory limitations, selective attention, belief biases) constrain the logicality of the observed behaviour. The application of this distinction varies markedly between theorists, however.

Inference rule theorists, for example, identify reasoning competence in the possession of a set of general purpose abstract logical (or quasi-logical) rules. This approach has a similarity to the "weak methods" problem solving theory of Newell and Simon and a computer model of deduction implemented by Rips (1983) is open to similar criticisms to those given earlier. The particular problem that inference rule theorists face is the explanation of the substantial effects of problem content on subjects' appraisal of logically equivalent arguments. The performance component must largely reflect interpretational problems in the representation of problem information.

Heuristic approaches have been aimed at the explanation of the many experimentally demonstrated errors and biases arising from both the presentation and content of problems. For example, Pollard (1982) has argued that the availability heuristic (originally applied to statistical judgement by Tversky & Kahneman, 1973) can explain errors since responses are dominated by the problem features made salient by their presentation or by available cues retrieved from memory. Evans (1984) has argued for a distinction between *heuristic* processes responsible for selective representation of problem content as "relevant" and *analytic* processes which generate inferences from these representations. Both theorists have, however, emphasised the explanation of biases rather than proposing mechanisms for reasoning competence.

schema theorists argue that reasoning performance reflects not general purpose inference rules, but rather the operation of production rules embedded within pragmatic reasoning schemas (see for an example Cheng and Holyoak, 1985, and for a review, Holland, Holyoak, Nisbett & Thagard, 1986, Chapter 9). Such theories are well suited to the explanation of the influence that problem content and context have on logical reasoning performance, but lack an apparent mechanism for explaining the significant logical competence that people can still exhibit with artificial or arbitrary problem content (Johnson-Laird, personal communication). Also particularly interesting is the notion that reasoning reflects the construction and manipulation of mental models to represent possible states of affairs suggested by the premises of the argument (Johnson-Laird, 1983; Johnson-Laird & Bara, 1984) a theory which is also opposed to the proposal of general purpose inference rules.

mental models theory provides a mechanism for deductive competence which is purely semantic. For example, given a syllogism of the kind mentioned earlier, the theory says that subjects will construct alternative possible models of the world in which the premises are true. If they fail to find a *counter-example*, i.e. a model in which the conclusion is false, then they regard the argument as valid. The belief bias effect, demonstrated by Evans et al (among others) can be explained in the performance component of this theory. For example, when the conclusion is believable, as in the example, subjects may lack motivation to conduct an exhaustive search and fail to find a counter-example (see Oakhill & Johnson-Laird, 1985). Errors on artificial reasoning problems are explained principally in terms of working memory capacity; subjects are assumed to have problems when several alternative models need to be constructed and compared (see Johnson-Laird & Bara, 1984).

Finally, in this section, we should record that contemporary studies of reasoning owe a great debt to the work of a highly creative British psychologist, Peter Wason. In the 1960s Wason invented two reasoning tasks which investigated a person's ability to test hypotheses in the context of deductive and inductive reasoning. These two tasks are known as the four card or "selection" task and the "2–4–6" problem respectively (see Wason & Johnson-Laird, 1972). Both tasks have stimulated, and continue to provoke an enormous amount of research. The selection task has been a particular vehicle for the investigation of the facilitatory effects of problem content (see Griggs, 1983; Wason, 1983) whilst the 2–4–6 problem has been heavily used in studies of the claim that rule learning strategies are dominated by a "confirmation bias" (see, for example, Tweney et al, 1980; Gorman, Stafford & Gorman, 1987). A British tradition has been maintained with the work of Wason's students, including Johnson-Laird and myself, and of course that of our own students and other colleagues.

3 Decision Making and Judgement

Decision making is an interdisciplinary field involving a grouping of disciplines (economics, business studies, management science etc.) different both in character and objective to those involved in cognitive science. Psychologists in this field are principally engaged in one of two (closely related) activities: *decision analysis* (see von Winterfeldt & Edwards, 1986), and empirical investigation of behavioural decision making and judgement (see Wright, 1984, for an introduction).

There is a rather hazy distinction between the formal, prescriptive decision theory underlying decision analysis and the attempts of psychologists to provide descriptive models of human decision behaviour, with the term *behavioural decision theory* being applied rather loosely to cover both approaches. The study of intuitive judgement (particularly statistical judgement) has emerged as an important subdiscipline for the simple reason that judgements and forecasts of uncertain events are an essential part of decision making, in which the consequences of actions must be projected and evaluated. European psychologists are strongly represented in contemporary studies of decision making as inspection of the contents of several recent edited volumes reveals (see Humphreys, Svenson & Vari, 1983; Sjoberg, Tyszka & Wise, 1983; Wright, 1985; Wright & Ayton, 1987). The European journal *Acta Psychologica* is also one of the major outlets for work in this area.

A brief historical review is essential to understand the similarities and differences of psychological work in this area to that in problem solving and reasoning. Modern decision theory has its roots in the work of von Neumann & Morgenstern (1947) who developed mathematical game theory as a model of economic behaviour. The notion of fundamental importance was that a rational individual should act in such a way as to maximise expected utility (subjective value) by taking into account the probabilities of alternative possible consequences of decision acts. The relevance of this work to psychology was spotted by Ward Edwards who spread the interest from its economic base by the writing of two major and influential review articles (Edwards, 1954; 1961). Edwards was also responsible for developing the idea that probabilities as well as utilities should be treated in a subjective manner, an approach facilitated by parallel development of psychological interest in Bayesian statistics.

The current normative decision theory is hence based upon the notion that people maximise *subjective* expected utility and it is generally known by the acronym SEU. An important extension of the theory permits expected utilities to be aggregated across multiple dimensions or attributes which bear upon evaluation of a decision; an extension known as multi-attribute utility theory (MAUT). A number of psychologists, including Edwards, have maintained an active role in decision analysis, which involves application of prescriptive decision theory to the solution of real world problems. Several significant psychological problems arise in the course of decision analysis. First of all the problem must be structured; that is, the decision maker must be assisted in identifying the options available and in projecting and evaluating the possible consequences of any choices taken. Practitioners appear to regard this structuring stage as the most important part of decision analysis (see, for example, von Winterfeldt & Edwards, 1986; Berkeley & Humphreys, 1982). However, in order to apply a decision theoretic analysis, methods have also been required for the tricky problem of elicitation of subjective probability and utility estimates.

An interesting development from the decision analysis approach is that of automated decision aids (see Wishuda, 1985), principally implemented as computer programs. There is currently much software available described as "decision support systems", e.g. for assisting financial decision making, which informs decision making by providing access to relevant databases and/or by computational modelling of the consequences of actions. There are also some expert consultant systems which are AI programs designed to replace human experts and perform a consultative role in narrow and well defined areas (see Hayes-Roth, Waterman & Lenat, 1983). It is, however, likely that there will also be considerable development of software in the near future which aims to automate traditional decision analysis in terms of problem structuring and offering decision theoretic recommendations. A pioneering program of this kind called MAUD was devised by the British Psychologist Patrick Humphreys some years ago and has undergone several updates. For psychological evaluations of MAUD and comparisons with conventional decision analysis see Humphreys & McFadden (1980) and John, von Winterfeldt & Edwards (1983).

Behavioural decision theory, in the descriptive sense of the term, has its origins in the same tradition. Indeed, a number of efforts were made to demonstrate the effectiveness of SEU as a descriptive model, although this ultimately failed (see Slovic, Fischhoff & Lichtenstein, 1977) and has inspired the proposal of a major alternative theory of risky decision making, known as *prospect theory* (Kahneman & Tversky, 1979). More importantly, however, the past 15 to 20 years has seen a major effort of psychological experimentation on judgement under uncertainty which has provided extensive evidence of errors and bias. This work is seen by many as a threat to the practice of decision analysis with its emphasis upon the rational nature of subjective judgement in decision making. It is not surprising therefore that hostile reactions to the studies of judgemental bias have appeared in some recent publications (see, for example, Berkeley & Humphreys, 1982; Beach, Christensen-Szalanski & Barnes, 1987) with criticisms aimed at both methodology and interpretation.

The theoretical driving force behind the work on bias in judgement is largely attributable to the collaborative work of two psychologists Daniel Kahneman and Amos Tversky who have published a series of highly prestigious theoretical papers since the early 1970s proposing the use of judgemental heuristics which often lead to serious and systematic biases. For example, the "availability" heuristic is a proposed mechanism by which people judge the likelihood of an event by the ease with which they can call examples to mind. Such a heuristic may often function adequately but can also lead to systematic bias, for a number of reasons. Events which are more accessible in the cognitive organisation of memory, favoured by primacy or recency effects, more "vivid" (cf. Nisbett & Ross, 1980), more conducive to prior beliefs and expectations and so on, may be available in disproportion to their true frequency. Such factors are claimed to lead not just to random error, but to systematic and predictable biases.

The "heuristics and biases" approach, as it has become known, has been supported by a large amount of psychological experimentation, particularly in the area of statistical judgement. A representative collection of work in this tradition is to be found in the collection of papers edited by Kahneman, Slovic and Tversky (1982) and a very interesting exposition of its impact on cognitive social psychology is given by Nisbett and Ross (1980).

To illustrate both the theoretical issues and practical implications involved in the decision and judgement area let us consider briefly the problem of medical diagnosis. A medical expert observes evidence in the form of symptom reports, test results or examinations, on the basis of which a diagnosis of the underlying cause, illness or condition must be made. This is, in fact, a statistical decision process of classic Bayesian characteristics. The posterior odds in favour of the condition considered (i.e. odds after viewing the evidence) are a function of both the prior odds (or *base rate*) and the likelihood ratio or *diagnosticity* of the evidence. The base rate probability of a patient suffering from a condition is relative to knowledge about the patient. For example, the prior probability of a heart attack in someone who is male, middle-aged, overweight and a heavy smoker is considerably higher than that of the average member of the population. Base rate data are relevant unless the evidence is 100% diagnostic, which it rarely is. Formally, the diagnosticity of the evidence refers to the likelihood that it could arise due to the suspected cause relative to the likelihood that it could arise from any other cause.

The Bayesian analysis of probability assessment is, however, only part of what is required to make a rational decision. The other requirement is a cost-benefit analysis in which the utilities associated with alternative outcomes must be considered. For example, universal testing for a rare medical condition may be justified if the cost of testing is small, but the consequences of failing to detect the condition may be very high for the individuals affected. In view of all this, should we be worried that medical diagnosis is often left to the unaided "intuitive" judgement of the experts concerned?

The results of psychological experimentation in this area should indeed give rise to concern. Base rate data, for example, have been widely shown to be neglected altogether by subjects making intuitive probability judgements in a large number of experiments, although there are some conditions in which they may be taken into account (see Bar-Hillel, 1980; Pollard & Evans, 1983). It has been specifically suggested that this kind of faulty statistical reasoning can lead physicians to make irrational decisions, for example to recommend unjustified investigative surgery (e.g. see Eddy, 1982). There is also much cause for concern with regard to the perception of the diagnosticity of evidence. Two major sources of error demonstrated in the literature on reasoning and judgement are "confirmation bias" and "belief bias" (discussed by Evans, 1987). The former refers to a tendency to seek evidence which conforms with prior expectations and the latter to biased evaluation and assimilation of evidence presented. Again, the existence of these biases in medical and other expert populations has been demonstrated.

Finally, in this section, I should mention that some work of contemporary psychologists in decision making is adopting a more "cognitive" approach than has been traditionally followed and is hence making contact with some of the theoretical issues discussed earlier with reference to problem solving and reasoning. For example, the importance of understanding the mental representations of decision problems is emphasised in recent work by Humphreys & Berkeley (e.g. 1985). There is interest in efforts to trace the thought processes underlying decision making by using methods such as verbal protocol analysis (Svenson, 1979; 1983). The mental models approach is also being investigated and appears to provide a good basis for theorising about the psychological mechanisms for forecasting and assessment of uncertain possibilities by reference to the use of "mental simulations" and the construction and comparison of alternative scenarios (see Kahneman & Tversky, 1982; Jungermann & Thuring, 1987; Vlek & Otten, 1987).

DISCUSSION AND NEW DIRECTIONS

In this, final, section of the chapter I will try to identify some of the salient issues arising from the review which will shape future research on higher cognitive processes. As may be inferred from the structure of this chapter, I believe this process would benefit from greater interchange and collaboration between researchers in the different traditions identified above. The Plymouth group has already attempted some degree of integration in recent years by pursuing and publishing research into both deductive reasoning and statistical judgement with much cross referencing of the two literatures. We also hosted an international workshop on Reasoning, Decision and Judgement in January 1984 where leading researchers from the different fields were brought together. The workshop led to a clear consensus that common issues underlie the research efforts of these differing traditions.

With reference to specific theoretical issues, it is interesting to note a parallel development in the fields of problem solving, reasoning and artificial intelligence alluded to. In each of these fields a theoretical shift has taken place over the past twenty years from a predominantly general purpose notion of intelligence (weak methods, logical inference rules etc.) towards a much more domain sensitive concept of schemas, mental models and expert system databases. One of the consequences of this shift is that the interests of researchers in the fields of thinking and memory have converged quite markedly. The move towards a knowledge based concept of intelligence has meant that memory researchers have proposed much more active dynamic models than the earlier static notions of memory stores, whilst reasoning researchers have become more interested in exploring representational concepts such as schemas and mental models. However, these approaches are relatively new and further theoretical and experimental work on the relation between knowledge structures and inferencing mechanisms should be a major priority in the next few years.

One of the difficulties concerning this issue and reasoning research generally is the task dependent nature of many findings. For example, two theoretical approaches to inference which clearly require further study are those based upon schema theory and mental models. Although couched as general theories, most of the evidence for the former currently rests upon studies of content effects in the Wason selection task whilst the latter approach has been tested almost entirely in the domain of categorical syllogisms. Neither theory is particularly well equipped to explain the sorts of findings to which the other has been applied (see Evans, 1989). Experimental study of both of these theories over a wider range of tasks and domains is clearly needed. However, simple empiricism will not suffice in the absence of conceptual clarifications. Both the schema and mental models concepts are frequently criticised for a certain vagueness in their definition.

An apparently distinct problem highlighted by comparison of work on reasoning and judgement is that of bias. In addition to the obvious practical importance of understanding why biases occur and how they can be reduced or eliminated, there are a number of important theoretical questions to be resolved. There is actually a complementary relationship between this work and that on the possible mechanisms of inference discussed above. The orientation of one approach is to the explanation of how people are able to reason successfully, whilst the other is concerned with understanding of how and why inference apparently fails.

The Kahneman & Tversky theory of judgemental heuristics is in effect a theory of general purpose reasoning mechanisms with emphasis on their limitations (the shady side of weak methods, if you like). Other researchers, however, have emphasised much more specific causes of bias, identifying them with aspects of both the presentation and content of particular task designs. Hence, the "non-reasoning" research involves a similar general versus specific debate to that involved in reasoning theory. There is also a major theoretical issue concerning the reason that successful reasoning and bias are so often manifest in combination in subjects' performance of experimental tasks. One view is that reasoning mechanisms are inherently rational and effective, but form only a competence system subject to performance factors. An opposing view is that inferential mechanisms are inherently flawed and inevitably generate mixed results. Resolution of this issue is essential, if the development of "debiasing" procedures is to have a sound theoretical basis.

Let us now consider some more applied issues that must be addressed by psychologists interested in the higher cognitive processes. I feel that the state of cognitive theory is now sufficiently advanced that attempts to apply the insights gained to real world problems can be made. Equally, I believe that the results of such attempts can only help us to develop our theoretical knowledge, for example by broadening the domains of study as suggested above. I have space here to outline two principal types of application that I feel we should be pursuing which I will label roughly as "knowledge elicitation" and "debiasing".

Knowledge elicitation is a problem which has been highlighted by recent developments in expert system technology and "knowledge engineering" (see, for example, Gammack & Young, 1984; Hart, 1985). Since such systems aim to embody the wisdom of a human expert it has proved necessary to attempt to externalise that knowledge by eliciting it from a human expert. This has proved to be very difficult because, for example, human databases appear to be huge in size and very complex in structure. More directly relevant to the topic of this chapter is the fact that much procedural knowledge (knowing how to do things) appears to be implicit and inaccessible to verbal report (see the section on problem solving).

Elsewhere (Evans, 1988) I have considered at length the potential contribution of cognitive psychology to this problem. I have suggested that there are three main types of knowledge that we can bring to this problem:

1. An understanding of the nature of knowledge representation in humans.
2. Knowledge of the cognitive limitations and biases which will constrain the exhibition of reasoning competence.
3. Experience in the application of alternative methodologies, such as protocol analysis, for discovering the nature of people's cognitive processes.

The knowledge elicitation problem has ramifications beyond the problems of knowledge engineers, however. For example, the development of sophisticated training procedures would be greatly facilitated by more explicit understanding of what constitutes expert knowledge in the domain of application. If we could measure the knowledge (not just the performance) of experts and trainees we would be better equipped to decide which training methods were more or less effective and which trainees were most likely to benefit from training. To take a further example from my own current experience, I am involved in an interdisciplinary project with computer scientists and engineers which aims to develop an intelligent interactive design aid. The psychologists were called in because the engineers realised that they did not actually know how they design things and wanted us to study them and find out! I suspect that this is fairly typical of the increasing practical demands that will be made on cognitive psychologists over the next few years.

The debiasing problem is not entirely separate. For example, if we could sort the biases out from the more efficient aspects of expert thinking *before* programming the expert system this would constitute a kind of debiasing. However, two distinct areas of application concern education and training on the one hand, and development of decision and design aids on the other. The first of these involves the idea that reasoning biases might be avoided by appropriate training. Such work as has been carried out so far has produced rather equivocal results.

For example, the use of verbal instructions which explain logical principles and emphasise the importance of their application are not generally very effective in improving deductive reasoning performance. Barston (1986, Experiments 6 to 9), for example, made a series of unsuccessful attempts to remove belief bias effects by such means. A recent study by Cheng, Holyoak, Nisbett & Oliver (1986) also found little benefit on deductive reasoning performance of either laboratory training in logical principles or prior attendance at logic classes. They did, however, find that training in the use of relevant pragmatic reasoning schemas produced a major facilitation of performance.

Some work on training of statistical judgements and inferences, however, has proved more encouraging. For example, feedback training can improve the accuracy of likelihood judgements made repetitively (Lichtenstein & Fischhoff, 1980). Fong, Krantz & Nisbett (1986) were able to show benefits for statistical reasoning from general training in statistical principles such as the law of large numbers in the laboratory as well as benefits from attendance at statistics classes. The contrast with the logical reasoning studies has led some of the authors involved to a rather curious hybrid theory in which inference rules are proposed for statistical but not logical reasoning (see Holland, Holyoak, Nisbett & Thagard, 1986, Chapter 9). There are clearly theoretical as well as applied motives for pursuing further research on this topic.

Developments in new technology are causing cognitive psychologists to become increasingly involved in the design, development and evaluation of a variety of types of interactive software. In addition to expert systems, current developments include computer assisted instruction and training, automated assessment of cognitive abilities and a variety of design and decision aids. As such programs become increasingly sophisticated and "intelligent" they will possess as a common feature the need to model the human being using the problem. In fact, such systems may need to have models of the problem domain, the subject's problem, the subject's own knowledge and limitations and also of the individual's actual decision process. Psychological issues arise both in understanding the likely nature of the human user's knowledge and thought processes in the domain of application, and also in the design and evaluation of the user interface characteristics of the system (see Norman & Draper, 1986).

I personally see the development of interactive design and decision aids as an important means of debiasing decision making by, for example, replacing otherwise biased intuitive judgements using accurate computational and database search methods (where possible), by the design of the user interface to ensure attention to relevant information and prompting for forgetting of earlier decisions, by assisting the user in structuring the problem and by application of decision theoretic methods. In this respect I am rather perturbed by the frequently negative reaction of psychologists in the decision analysis tradition to the accumulated evidence of judgemental biases. However, I also believe that interactive (and intelligent) decision aids are likely to involve much more than simple automation of traditional decision analysis methods.

It is to be hoped that those authors now taking a greater interest in the application of cognitive models to decision making (cf. the end of the previous section) are on a converging course with those from a background in problem solving and reasoning who are seeking applications of their theoretical knowledge to real world problems.

REFERENCES

Bar-Hillel, M. (1980) The base-rate fallacy in probability judgements. *Acta Psychologica*, 44, 211-233.

Barston. J.l. (1986) 'An investigation into belief biases in reasoning.' Unpublished Ph.D. thesis, Plymouth Polytechnic.

Beach, L.R., Christensen-Szalanski, J. & Barnes, V. (1987) Assessing human judgement: Has it been done, can it be done, should it be done? In G. Wright & P. Ayton (Eds) *Judgemental Forecasting*. Chichester: Wiley.

Berkeley, D. & Humphreys, P. (1982) Structuring decision problems and the bias heuristic. *Acta Psychologica*, 50, 201-252.

Berry, D.C. & Broadbent, D.E. (1984) On the relationship between task performance and associated verbalizable knowledge. *Quarterly Journal of Experimental Psychology*, 36A, 209-231.

Broadbent, D.E., Fitzgerald, P, & Broadbent, M.H.P. (1986) Implicit and explicit knowledge in the control of complex systems. *British Journal of Psychology*, 77, 33-50.

Cheng, P.W. & Holyoak, K.J. (1985) *Pragmatic reasoning schemas. Cognitive Psychology*, 17, 391-416.

Cheng, P.W., Holyoak, K.J., Nisbett, R.E. & Oliver, L.M. (1986) *Pragmatic versus syntactic approaches to training deductive reasoning. Cognitive Psychology*, 18, 293-328.

Cohen, L.J. (1981) Can human irrationality be experimentally demonstrated? *The Behavioral and Brain Sciences*, 4, 317-370.

Duncker,K. (1945) On problem solving. *Psychological Monographs*, 1945, 58, Whole no 270.

Eddy, D.M. (1982) Probabilistic reasoning in clinical medicine: Problems and opportunities. In D. Kahneman, P. Slovic and A. Tversky (eds) *Judgment Under Uncertainty: Heuristics and Biases*. Cambridge: Cambridge University

Edwards, W. (1954) The theory of decision making. *Psychological Bulletin*, 41, 380-417.

Edwards, W. (1961) Behavioral Decision Theory. *Annual Review of Psychology*, 67, 441-52.

Ericsson, K.A. & Simon, H.A. (1980) Verbal reports as data. *Psychological Review*, 87, 215-251.

Ericsson, K.A. & Simon, H.A. (1984) *Protocol Analysis: Verbal reports as data*. Cambridge, Mass.: M.I.T. Press.

Evans, J.St.B.T. (1982) *The Psychology of Deductive Reasoning*. London: Routledge and Kegan Paul.

Evans, J.St.B.T. (1984) Heuristic and analytic processes in reasoning. *British Journal of Psychology*, 75, 451-468.

Evans, J.St.B.T. (1987) Beliefs and expectations as causes of judgemental bias. In G. Wright & P. Ayton (eds) *Judgemental Forecasting*. Wiley.

Evans, J.St.B.T. (1988) The knowledge elicitation problem: a psychological perspective. *Behaviour and Information Technology* , 7, 111-130.

Evans, J.St.B.T. (1989) *Bias in Human Reasoning: Causes and consequences*. London: Lawrence Erlbaum Associates Ltd.

Evans, J.St.B.T., Barston, J.L. & Pollard, P. (1983) On the conflict between logic and belief in syllogistic reasoning. *Memory and Cognition*, 11, 295-306.

Fong, G.T., Krantz, D.H. & Nisbett, R.E. (1986) The effects of statistical training on thinking about everyday problems. *Cognitive Psychology*, 18, 253-292.

Gammack, J.G. & Young, R.M. (1984) Psychological techniques for eliciting expert knowledge. In M.A. Bramer (ed) *Research and Development in Expert Systems*. Cambridge: Cambridge University Press.

Gick, M.L. & Holyoak, K.J. (1980) Analogical problem solving. *Cognitive Psychology*, 12, 306-355.

Gick, M.L. & Holyoak, K.J. (1983) Schema induction and analogical transfer. *Cognitive Psychology*, 15, 1-38.

Gilhooly, K.J.G. (1982) *Thinking: Directed, Undirected and Creative*. London: Academic Press.

Gorman, M.E., Stafford, A. & Gorman, M.E. (1987) Disconfirmation and dual hypotheses on a more difficult version of Wason's 2-4-6 task. *Quarterly Journal of Experimental Psychology*, 39A, 1-28.

Griggs, R.A. (1983) The role of problem content in the selection task and in the THOG problem. In J.St.B.T. Evans (ed) *Thinking and Reasoning: Psychological Approaches*. London: Routledge and Kegan Paul.

Hart, A. (1985) The role of induction in knowledge elicitation. *Expert Systems*, 2, 24-28.

Hayes-Roth, F. Waterman, D.A. & Lenat, D.B. (1983) *Building Expert Systems*. London: Addison-Wesley.

Henle, M. (1962) On the relation between logic and thinking. *Psychological Review*, 69, 366-378.

Holland, J.H., Holyoak, K.J., Nisbett, R.E. & Thagard, P.R. (1986) *Induction: Processes of Inference, Learning and Discovery*. Cambridge, Mass.: MIT Press.

Humphreys, P. & Berkeley, D. (1985) Handling uncertainty: Levels of analysis of decision problems. In G. Wright (Ed) *Behavioral Decision Making*. New York: Plenum Press.

Humphreys, P., Svenson, O. & Vari, A. (Eds) (1983) *Analysing and Aiding Decision Processes*. Amsterdam: North Holland.

Humphreys, P.C. & McFadden, W. (1980) Experiences with MAUD: Aiding decision structuring versus bootstrapping the decision maker. *Acta Psychologica*, 45, 51-69.

Inhelder, B. & Piaget, J. (1958) *The Growth of Logical Thinking*. New York: Basic Books.

John, R.S., von Winterfeldt, D. & Edwards, W. (1983). The quality and user acceptance of multiattribute utility analysis performed by computer and analyst. In Humphreys, P., Svenson, O. & Vari, A. (1983). *Analysing and Aiding Decision Processes*. Amsterdam: North Holland.

Johnson-Laird, P.N. (1983) *Mental Models*. Cambridge: Cambridge University Press.

Johnson-Laird, P.N. & Bara, B.G. (1984) *Syllogistic Inference. Cognition*, 16, 1-62.

Jungermann, H. & Thuring, M. (1987) The use of mental models for generating scenarios. In G. Wright and P. Ayton (eds) *Judgemental Forecasting*. Chichester: Wiley. @REFS = Kahneman, D. & Tversky, A. (1979) Prospect theory: An analysis of decision under risk. *Econometrica*, 47, 263-291.

Kahneman, D. & Tversky, A. (1982) The simulation heuristic. In A. Kahneman, P. Slovic & A. Tversky (eds) *Judgment Under Uncertainty: Heuristics and Biases*. Cambridge: Cambridge University Press.

Kahneman, D., Slovic, P. & Tversky, A. (1982) *Judgment Under Uncertainty: Heuristics and Biases*. Cambridge: Cambridge University Press.

Kahney, H. (1986) *Problem Solving: A Cognitive Approach*. Milton Keynes: Open University Press.

Keane, M.T. (1988) *Analogical Problem Solving*. Chichester: Horwood.

Lichtenstein, S. & Fischhoff, B. (1980) Training for calibration. *Organisational Behaviour and Human Performance*, 26, 149-171.

Luchins, A.S. (1942) Mechanisation in problem solving. *Psychological Monographs*, 54, Whole no 248.

Mandler, J.M. & Mandler, G. (1964) *Thinking: From Association to Gestalt*. New York: Wiley.

Mayer, R.E. (1983) *Thinking, Problem Solving, Cognition*. U.S.A.: Freeman.

Newell, A. & Simon, H.A. (1972) *Human problem solving*. Englewood Cliffs, N.J.: Prentice-Hall.

Nisbett, R. & Ross, L. (1980) *Human inference: Strategies and Shortcomings of Social Judgement*. Englewood Cliffs, N.J.: Prentice-Hall.

Nisbett, R.E. & Wilson, T.D. (1977) Telling more than we can know: Verbal reports on mental processes. *Psychological Review*, 84, 231-295.

Norman, D.A. & Draper, S.W. (1986) *User Centered System Design*. Hillsdale, N.J.: Erlbaum.

Oakhill, J. & Johnson-Laird, P.N. (1985) The effect of belief on the spontaneous production of syllogistic conclusions. *Quarterly Journal of Experimental Psychology*, 37A, 553-570.

Pollard, P. (1982) *Human reasoning: some possible effects of availability. Cognition*, 12, 65-96.

Pollard, P. & Evans, J.St.B.T. (1983) The role of representativeness in statistical inference: A critical appraisal. In J.St.B.T. Evans (ed), *Thinking and reasoning: Psychological approaches*. London: Routledge & Kegan Paul.

Reber, A.S., Kassin, S.M., Lewis, S. & Cantor, G. (1980) On the relationship between implicit and explicit modes in the learning of a complex rule structure. *Journal of Experimental Psychology:*

Human Learning and Memory, 6, 492-502.

Rips, L.J. (1983) Cognitive processes in propositional reasoning. *Psychological Review*, 90, 38-71.

Rumelhart, D.E. (1980) Schemata: The building blocks of cognition. In R.J. Spiro, B.C. Bruce & W.F. Brewer (eds) *Theoretical Issues in Reading Comprehension*. Hillsdale, N.J.: Erlbaum.

Sjoberg, L., Tyszka, T. & Wise, J.A. (1983) *Human Decision Making*. Sweden: Doxa.

Slovic, P., Fischhoff, B. & Lichtenstein, S. (1977) Behavioral decision theory. *Annual Review of Psychology*, 228, 1-39.

Svenson, O. (1979) Process descriptions of decision making. *Organisational Behavior and Human Performance*, 23, 86-112.

Svenson, O. (1983) Scaling evaluative statements in verbal protocols from decision processes. In P. Humphreys, O. Svenson & A. Vari (Eds) *Analysing and Aiding Decision Processes*. Amsterdam: North Holland.

Tversky, A. & Kahneman, D. (1973). Availability: A heuristic for judging frequency and probability. *Cognitive Psychology*, 5, 207-232

Tweney, R.D., Doherty, M.E., Warner, W.J., Pliske, D.B., Mynatt, (1980) Strategies of rule discovery in an inference task. *Quarterly Journal of Experimental Psychology*, 32, 109-24.

Vlek, C. & Otten, W. (1987) Judgemental handling of energy scenarios: A psychological analysis and experiment. In G. Wright & P. Ayton (Eds) *Judgmental Forecasting*. Chichester: Wiley.

von Neumann, J. & Morgenstern, O. (1947) *Theory of games and economic behavior*. Princeton, N.J.: Princeton University Press.

von Winterfeldt, D. & Edwards, W. (1986) *Decision Analysis and Behavioural Research*. Cambridge: Cambridge University Press.

Wason, P.C. (1983) Realism and rationality in the selection task. In J. St.B. T. Evans (ed), *Thinking and Reasoning: Psychological Approaches*. London: Routledge & Kegan Paul.

Wason, P.C. & Johnson-Laird, P.N. (1972) *Psychology of Reasoning: Structure and Content*. London: Batsford.

Wertheimer, M. (1961) *Productive Thinking*. London: Tavistock.

White, P.A. (1988) Knowing more than we can tell: 'Introspective access' and causal report accuracy 10 years later. *British Journal of Psychology*, 79, 13-46.

Wishuda, A.D. (1985) Design of decision-aiding systems. In G. Wright (Ed) *Behavioral Decision Making*. New York: Plenum Press.

Wright, G. (1984) *Behavioural Decision Theory*. Harmandsworth: Penguin.

Wright, G. & Ayton, P. (1987) *Judgemental Forecasting*. Chichester: Wiley.

Wright, G.N. (1985) (ed) *Behavioural Decision Making*. New York: Plenum.

CHAPTER 6

Psycholinguistics: Some Research Issues

L.G.M.Noordman

*Department of Psychology, Tilburg University,
The Netherlands*

The object of study in psycholinguistics is the human language processing system. The aim of the research is to explain the cognitive processes of language production and comprehension in communication, and to account for the acquisition of language production and comprehension skills. Psycholinguistics is properly a subfield of cognitive psychology, and not, despite the morphology of its name in English, of linguistics. Although there may be a close interaction between linguistics and psycholinguistics, a careful distinction should be made between the two disciplines. They have different objectives and different methodologies. A linguist tries to account for the structural properties of language at the different levels of the language such as the semantic, syntactic, phonological, morphological and phonetic level. In syntax, for example, a linguist tries to formulate rules so as to account for the grammaticality of the sentences of the language. In morphology the rules that are developed aim at defining the well-formedness of morphological structures. A linguistic theory may consist of representations and processes, but these aim to describe and to derive the structural properties of the language system.

Psycholinguists, on the other hand, address themselves to language behavior. The rules developed by psycholinguists aim to describe the mental processes of producing language, understanding language and the acquisition of language. Language behavior no doubt involves processes at the different linguistic levels that can be distinguished in language, but there is no *a priori* reason to suppose that the processes described in linguistic theory are cognitive processes in actual language use. A psycholinguist working on syntax is interested in the way in which syntactic structures are derived in real time in language understanding and how they are generated in real time in language production. Psycholinguistic research with respect to morphology addresses the question of how morphologically complex words are represented in the mental lexicon and how the entries are accessed. There is no *a priori* reason to assume that the most parsimonious linguistic description of morphological structure corresponds to the cognitive representation of morphological structure that is used in real time processes.

In order to study language behavior psycholinguists have developed several research methods. The cognitive processes involved in language production and comprehension, like all cognitive processes, are to a large extent inaccessible to direct observation. Thus psycholinguistics has been forced to resort to various indirect measures from which conclusions about the nature of the underlying processes may be drawn. These measures fall into several major groups. A distinction that is frequently made is between on-line and off-line tasks. In an on-line task the measurement is as closely in time as possible to the processing. In many cases the data are measures of response times. An example is the lexical decision task. Subjects have to decide whether a presented sequence of letters or sounds forms a word. By varying the words that are presented with respect to particular properties (e.g. morphological complexity, (word frequency), differences in response time are interpreted as reflecting temporal characteristics of the processing of the experimental variable that is manipulated. reading times per sentence and durations of eye fixations are other examples. Other tasks measure the time needed to detect a particular target, e.g., a tone or a pre-specified letter within the material presented for comprehension. The detection time in these so-called double tasks reflects the cognitive effort involved in processing the material presented and therefore the underlying processes.

It should not be thought that only response time studies address the temporal characteristics of language processing. Studies in which the input is "under control of the experimenter" address this issue even when no response times are measured. An example is the gating task in auditory word recognition in which incremental segments of a word are presented for recognition. In these cases the type of response can lead to inferences about the course of processing in time.

In off-line tasks there is a delay between the measurement and the processes that are investigated. Examples of off-line tasks are paraphrase tasks, which have been widely used in the study of ambiguity, for instance, various question-answering tasks, recall and recognition tasks which have been used in the study of the representation of the processed information.

The experimental study of language production encounters special difficulties, mainly due to lack of control of the experimental variables. Picture description tasks, without response time measurements, have been widely used in laboratory studies of language production. The difficulty of studying language production in the laboratory has, for instance, led to the examination of spontaneously occurring slips of the tongue. However, laboratory tasks have been developed in which slips of the tongue are experimentally elicited with a rather greater frequency than long-suffering production researchers have found them to occur in the wild.

The amount of research in psycholinguistics has increased considerably during the last decades. This has led to a better understanding of the fundamental problems that have to be solved by psycholinguistic research. This paper does not pretend to give a representative overview of the state of the art in psycholinguistics. It is not possible to do justice in a single chapter to the amount of research that is conducted in the different areas in psycholinguistics. A good and recent overview is Garnham (1985). The aim of this paper is to discuss certain important research topics in psycholinguistics focussing on the organization of the human language processing system. The selection of the topics that are discussed does not pretend to cover the whole field.

The paper is organized in different sections corresponding to the different processors involved in language production and comprehension. A consequence of this set-up is that there is no specific section on, for example, reading; research on reading is discussed in several sections. An overview of reading is given by Coltheart (1987a) and Just and Carpenter (1987).

The discussion of the human language processing system is followed by a short section which discusses the usefulness of cross-linguistic research. The last section discusses some language technological applications, the development of which requires fundamental psycholinguistic research.

Most of the research that is discussed has been conducted in laboratory experiments with normal subjects. Another way of investigating the functional architecture of the language processing system is to study the language impairment of patients with brain damage. Language disorders in neurologically damaged patients may be interpreted in terms of the breakdown of a particular subsystem or in terms of the breakdown of a particular connection between subsystems. This research is referred to as cognitive neuropsychology of language. It falls outside the scope of the present study. Neuropsychology is discussed in a separate chapter (see Volume Four). A recent overview of cognitive neuropsychology of language is Coltheart, Sartori, and Job (1987).

THE HUMAN LANGUAGE PROCESSING SYSTEM

The language user may be conceived of as a language processing system. This system consists of several interrelated subsystems or modules. Each subsystem is a specialist that fulfills a particular function by performing a particular kind of operation. The aim of psycholinguistic research is to specify this system, its subsystems and their relations.

The first task is to identify the different modules. Each module can be described at a computational level, an algorithmic level and an implementation level (Marr, 1982). At the computational level it should be specified what the goal of the computation is. At the algorithmic level one has to specify the input and output representations and the algorithms by which the transformations from the input representations to the output representations are accomplished. Finally it should be specified how the algorithm is implemented in the "hardware" in such a way that it can account for the real time characteristics of the process. This paper focusses on the algorithmic aspects of the language processing system.

In describing the different modules, some additional questions should be investigated. Is a process automatic, in the sense that it is not subject to capacity limitations, does not require awareness, and is not under strategic control, or is it controlled, in the sense that it is subject to limited capacity, requires attention and is under strategic control? With respect to the cooperation of the various subprocesses, a central question is whether these processes are autonomous in the sense that the different modules are connected with each other only by means of input and output channels, or whether there is an interactive influence of one process on the course of another process. Yet another question is whether the processes operate in parallel or serially.

These issues and questions form a list of topics on the research agenda, rather than a list of issues that have been settled.

The language processing system contains the following subsystems. There is a conceptualizer that plays a role in the production and comprehension of language. For the production of language there is a formulator and an articulator; for the comprehension of language there is a perceptual system and a comprehension system. The processes in the subsystems have access to two knowledge stores: the lexicon and world knowledge.

Conceptualizer

The conceptualizer contains a module for the generation of language, i.e. the generator, and a module for the interpretation of language, i.e. the interpreter. In addition, there is one for the control of the process, i.e. the monitor.

Generator

The input to the generator are the intentions and the conceptual information that the language user wants to communicate. The output is a preverbal, conceptual representation. In general, the input is a multidimensional structure, for example, a complex idea or a complex structure derived from perception. Such a structure may be considered as a mental model (Johnson-Laird, 1983) to be discussed later on. The information in such a structure is simultaneously available. The generator has to transform such a multidimensional structure into a one dimensional structure since the message is to be expressed in a linear string in time. Accordingly, the processes that are accomplished in the generator consist of the planning and selection of the information that is going to be expressed, and the lineariaztion of the information (Levelt, 1981).

The knowledge sources that are used by the generator include world knowledge, the knowledge about the discourse context and knowledge of what gets expressed in the language. Knowledge about the discourse context includes knowledge about the previous parts of the discourse, but also knowledge about the interlocutor or about the projected reader, in particular knowledge about the intentions, interests, and knowledge of the recipient. The speaker/writer has a conception of what the recipient already knows and wants to know. This is particularly clear in conversation. By knowledge about the language is meant that the language producer has to know (implicitly) what kind of information is required in using that particular language: what particular word forms, grammatical constructions and semantic distinctions are made in the particular language.

The processes in the conceptualizer are not automatic but under strategic control. They require attention and are subject to capacity limitations.

Exactly how these processes in the generator take place and how the knowledge is accessed and selected in these processes is still far from clear. Not only conceptual information can be the input to the language generator, but also perceptual information. The relation between language and perception (cf. scene descriptions, the semantics of spatial prepositions, multimodal communication; see the paper by Wahlster in Volume Two) is an important object of study. Furthermore, psycholinguistic research on the way in which language production processes are tuned to the listener/reader is still scarce, but it will be of great theoretical significance and of great value for the development of natural language interfaces.

Interpreter

The second processor in the conceptualizer is the interpreter. The input to the interpreter is the representation of the sentences delivered by the comprehension modules. The output is the representation of the conceptual information expressed in the discourse as well as the interpretation of the intentions of the speaker/writer. This representation will be referred to as the discourse representation, or mental model (Johnson-Laird, 1983; Garnham, 1987b). Two main questions with respect to this representation are: what is represented, and how is the representation constructed in the comprehension process?

With respect to the first question, it is clear that the representation contains more (or other) information than what is explicitly expressed in the uttered or written discourse. There is a variable relation between sentences as linguistic objects and their intended interpetations. In understanding the sequence:
We drove to the reception. On the way, the engine began to boil we certainly do not accept the semantic anomaly that the engine began to boil, but we understand that the cooling-water of the engine of the car started to boil. It is indeed not only the linguistic information that determines the representation; also contextual information and background knowledge are involved. Much information is implied and has to be derived in inference processes. Consider the following conversation between A and B.

A: *Do you know what time it is?*
B: *The mail has just been collected.*

These two utterances seem to be completely unrelated as far as the content of the sentences is concerned. Yet A will probably have no problem in figuring out how B's utterance is to be understood as an answer to the question. The implied information is deduced from the utterance, the discourse context and general knowledge.

There is an increasing interest in the study of discourse representation both from a psycholinguistic and linguistic point of view. From a psycholinguistic point of view one can say that the understanding of discourse consists in constructing a coherent representation of the information expressed and implied by the discourse. Both psycholinguists and linguists are concerned with the nature of these representations. Formal descriptions of discourse representations are developed in recent linguistic theories under different names, e.g. discourse representation (Kamp, 1981), context model (Bosch, 1983), discourse domain (Seuren, 1985), mental space (Fauconnier, 1985). (See also the chapter by Guenthner in Volume Two.) These approaches differ in some important aspects from traditional semantics which make them interesting from a psychological point of view. These discourse representations are cognitive representations of the information in the text, and not linguistic representations (cf. the example of the boiling engine). Furthermore, the representations are not static but dynamic. They are incrementally constructed. The linguistic expressions in the discourse are considered as instructions to construct a representation or to change the current representation. For example, an indefinite noun phrase may introduce a new element in the representation; the use of prepositional phrases may create a new subdomain. The meaning of a sentence (proposition) is considered as what the sentence contributes to the representation constructed so far. Another aspect refers to what the discourse representation has to account for. It should describe the conditions under which a discourse is true or false with respect to the world (or a model). But a truth conditional approach, in which the relation between discourse and a (world)model is specified, does not account for all aspects of meaning. The relation with a world is not the only relation that is important for the meaning of a text. Another aspect that has to be accounted for is the coherence of the discourse. It is not yet clear how the notion "coherence" should be formalized and how coherence may control inferencing. What has to be accounted for in describing coherence are the relations between representations. The advantages of these discourse theories, apart from their psychological attractiveness, is that they give a better account of some semantic phenomena such as presuppositions, and anaphora than traditional semantic theories.

The structure and coherence of a discourse representation not only depend on meaning relations between parts of the discourse, but also on relations between intentions of the writer and speaker (Grosz and Sidner, 1986). This is a promising area for future research. insight into this issue is also of particular importance for man-machine interfaces (see the chapter by Wahlster in Volume Two).

The state of our knowledge with respect to discourse representation lags far behind our knowledge with respect to sentence representation. Even the most basic questions regarding the nature of the representation are still problematic. The converging interest by linguists and psycholinguists on these issues opens interesting perspectives for collaborative research. But one should realize that it is an empirical question to what extent the linguistic models are indeed models of the processes and representations in the head of the language user.

The second question with respect to the discourse representation is how that representation is derived. From a psychological point of view one should describe how top-down factors such as knowledge and expectations of the reader with respect to the topic of the text, combine with bottom-up factors such as the specific cues in the text to construct the representation. A particular class of cues for the construction of a coherent representation are anaphoric expressions. The use of different kinds of anaphoric expressions, such as pronouns and definite noun phrases, depends on the role of the referred entity in the representation. For example, Sanford and Garrod (1981) claim that pronouns can only refer to entities in explicit focus, whereas definite noun phrases can refer to entities in explicit as well as in implicit focus. Therefore, pronouns or anaphoric expressions in general, contain information about the way in which the referred entities have to be searched for (Garnham, 1987a; Sidner, 1983).

A point of particular interest is how cues in the text come to activate and access world knowledge. One way in which this can be accomplished is that a word activates a particular script or schema. For example, the word *restaurant* may activate the restaurant script. But the relation between words and activated scripts is far from simple, as can be illustrated by an example from Riesbeck (1982): the program FRUMP summarized a story on *Pope's death shakes Western World* as : *There was an earthquake in the Western World; the Pope died.*

The representation depends to a large extent on inference processes. The control of inferencing is an important area for research. Inferences are made, but certainly not all the inferences are made that are possible. Textual factors and extra-textual factors, such as the knowledge and the goal of the reader, probably affect the on-line inference processes (Noordman and Vonk, 1987; Vonk, 1985). Related to this issue is the fact that understanding a text can mean very different things; the kinds of representation that are constructed can be very different. Psycholinguistic research should describe how these representations are produced.

Monitor

A third processor in the conceptualizer is the monitor. The monitor is the control function in the system. In language production, for example, the monitor compares the speaker's preverbal message with the postverbal message as analysed by the speaker on the basis of their own utterance (via overt speech or via internal feedback). A mismatch will enable the monitor to start some correction. In language understanding the monitor will signal when a particular utterance cannot be interpreted (unambiguously), or when it cannot be integrated with available knowledge.

One point that has to be studied is where the monitor is located in the model, or in other words, to which processes the monitor has access and where in the system there is a possibility for detecting errors. Levelt (1983; 1989) proposes a maximally parsimonious conception by locating the monitor exclusively in the conceptualizer. In other models, e.g. Kempen and Hoenkamp (1987), the monitor has access to the output of the various processors in language production.

Formulator

The conceptualizer determines what gets expressed, the specific form of the expressions depending to a large extent on the processes and constraints of the language modules down the line.

The input to the formulator are the conceptual representations that were the output of the generator. The output of the formulator consists of phonetic plans for the utterances. An influential model of language production, in particular of the formulator, is Garrett's (1975, 1980, 1982). Garrett identifies two subsystems within the formulator. The evidence for these subsystems comes mainly from speech errors, for example from the difference between sound exchange errors and word exchange errors. These errors are indeed subject to different distance constraints and similarity constraints. For example, word exchanges occur across constituent boundaries; sound exchanges occur between elements within a constituent. The words that exchange are in general words of the same syntactic class; sound exchanges occur between words of different syntactic classes. These and other observations lead to the assumption of two subsystems, one in which words are specified in terms of their syntactic characteristics, and one in which they are specified in terms of their phonological characteristics. The units in the first system correspond to a clause, those in the second system to a phrase. The representations that result from these subsystems are called functional level representation and positional level representation, respectively. A similar distinction is made by many other authors (Levelt, 1989; Kempen and Hoenkamp, 1987; Bock, 1987b). Following Levelt these processors will be called the grammatical encoder and the phonological encoder respectively.

Grammatical Encoder

The grammatical encoder receives as input the non-linguistic messages from the generator. Its output consists of a syntactic structure in which the grammatical relations are specified. What happens in this subsystem is that, on the basis of the conceptual information in the preverbal message, lexical items are accessed that are specified for semantic, syntactic and morphological information. (These lexical items are identified as lemmas by Kempen and Hoenkamp, in contrast to lexemes that are accessed in the phonological encoder.) This representation has all the information necessary to construct the serially ordered positional representation. As far as the nature of this representation is concerned, Garrett seems to leave open the possibility that this representation corresponds to an abstract or deep structure; many other authors (Levelt, Bock, Kempen and Hoenkamp) identify it as a surface structure.

Phonological Encoder

The phonological encoder receives as input the (surface) syntactic structure from the grammatical encoder. Its output is a string of syllables that are phonologically specified. This information serves as the input for the articulator. The processes at this level consist of the generation of a planning frame that specifies the word order, and the retrieval of lexical items (lexemes) that contain the form information, i.e., morphological, phonemic, metric and prosodic information.

The knowledge that is used by the formulator in transforming preverbal messages into the phonologically specified strings, is constituted by the different kinds of information retrieved from the lexicon. The processes involved in selecting lexical elements during language production and the role of syntactic and semantic constraints in these processes have hardly been investigated. One of the serious problems that has to be accounted for is how the process converges on the unique, correct word. Levelt (in press) calls this the criterion of correct convergence and suggests some principles that will guarantee the correct convergence in a model. Levelt and Flores d'Arcais (1987) show that a similar principle applies to comprehension. The problem in production is that when a particular meaning has to be expressed in a word, for example the concept *oak*, hypernyms of that word (tree) are activated as well. None of the existing models accounts for the unique selection of the correct word.

As far as the questions of automaticity and parallelism are concerned, it is hardly conceivable how the speaking process, rapid as it is, could take place, if these lexical retrieval processes were not automatic and parallel.

In the production model referred to above, two levels of lexical representations are distinguished. The question is what the structure of these representations looks like. There is not much evidence for an underlying deep structure in language production. Although Ford and Holmes (1978) and Ford (1982) showed that latencies for reactions to tones presented during sentence production, and pauses in spontaneous speech indicated the importance of deep structure, they argued that their data are also compatible with a semantic interpretation. On the other hand, there is strong evidence for a surface structure representation in sentence production. The occurrence of sound exchange errors and word exchange errors, referred to earlier, points to the role of a constituent structure and of a phrase structure in sentence production. Studies on repairs also provide evidence for the role of surface structure in production (Maclay and Osgood, 1959; Levelt, 1983, in terms of the rule of syntactic well-formedness; van Wijk and Kempen, 1987, in terms of the prosodic structure). Furthermore, the linguistic surface structure of a sentence seems to be a good predictor of the pause distribution in sentence production (Grosjean, Grosjean and Lane, 1979).

Although there is a great deal of evidence for the role of the syntactic surface structure in the organization of sentences, the question of how these structures are computed in sentence generation is still an open question. A model for sentence generation that is based on the computation of phrase structures (Yngve, 1960), is not very well supported. Van Wijk and Kempen (1982) did not obtain any evidence for syntactic computations in sentence generation. syntactic computations are presumably automatic processes. According to Bock (1987b): "The apparent automaticity and opacity of these processes indicates that it will take considerable ingenuity to break into the system that creates structure in speech".

The next module in speech production is the articulator. It transforms the phonetic plans into articulator motor instructions. Processes and representations in this module are discussed by Laver Volume Two of this series.

Relations between the Subsystems

A topic of research of the formulator is whether the two subsystems are autonomous modules, or whether there is some sort of interaction between them: whether there is feedback from the phonological encoder to the syntactic encoder. Garrett's model does not allow feedback from the lower level to the higher level. A weaker form of dependence is that the syntactic encoder produces multiple outputs from which the phonological encoder makes a selection.

There is some evidence that the two subsystems are not independent. Dell and Reich (1981) found phonological similarities in word exchanges, which is not permitted in an autonomous model, since word exchanges are supposed to take place at a "non-phonological" level of representation. Dell (1985, 1986) proposes an interactive model in which there are activation processes between the phonological elements and the words. Similarly, Stemberger (1985) argues on the basis of observed exchanges between inflectional morphemes for an interactive model.

Furthermore, Bock (1987a) observed that phonological activation affected the syntactic structure in sentence production. In a phonological priming task she found a small but significant preference for the phonologically primed word to serve as the object rather than as the subject of the sentences (phonological priming is an inhibitory effect). Bock (1987b) proposes a model which is very similar to Garrett's. She distinguishes between two levels of lexico-syntactic integration: functional integration and constituent integration. One of the main differences from Garrett's model is that the processes at both levels are influenced by the accessibility of the information, thus allowing for interaction between the levels. At the level of functional integration, for example, the first available noun is assigned to the subject role. At the constituent integration level phonologically accessible representations are assigned to earlier phrases. Sentences tend to be phrased in such a way that the phonologically accessible words appear early. Levelt and Maassen (1981) manipulated the accessibility of words in a free production experiment, and like Bock they found a small effect but this was not significant.

Given the available evidence, there seems to be feedback from phonological encoding to grammatical encoding. The question is what the nature of the feedback is: how do the lower level processes affect the higher level processes? Levelt (1989) offers a parsimonious interpretation of the feedback that accounts for the data in these experiments. When there is trouble in the phonological encoding (which may occur for example when a word is difficult to name or when a word is inhibited due to phonological priming) the encoding at the syntactic level may be revised.

In concluding this section on language production, it is appropriate to say that our present knowledge about language production is still very fragmentary. language production has been investigated less than language comprehension. This certainly depends in part on the difficulty of controlling the input of the system.

The Language Understanding System

The language understanding system, just as the production system, consists of several subsystems. In analysing speech, the first system, audition, converts physical sounds into phonetic representations by segmenting and categorising the continuous sounds into discrete phoneme-like units. Variation due to differences between speakers, dialect, tempo are no longer represented at this level. These issues are discussed in Chapter Three of this volume by Patterson and Cutler.

The first module in analysing written language is visual perception. The input in this module are visual shapes. The output is a representation of letter features, letters and letter strings. The processes and representations in this module are not discussed in this paper.

Phonological Decoding

The input to this system are the phonetic representations obtained from the audition module. The output consists of strings of lexical elements. Phonological decoding can also play a role in analyzing written language. A phonological representation of a written word may be obtained as a representation of the whole word, or may be obtained on the basis of grapheme-phoneme correspondence rules (discussed later).

The processes in this module are the segmentation of the stimulus and the identification of the words. Once a word is identified, its syntactic and semantic information is retrieved from the lexicon. A number of psycholinguistic models for lexical access and (oral and written) word recognition have been developed. The main variants are parallel activation models (Morton, 1969; Marslen-Wilson and Welsh, 1978; McClelland and Rumelhart, 1981) and search models (Forster, 1976).

One of the serious problems that has received relatively little attention in auditory word perception research is how word boundaries are determined. This question is related to the issue of morphological complexity. One of the problems in identifying words is not so much that the words presented have to be identified and accessed, but that all the other words have to be excluded. So the process has to converge to uniquely identify the target word. This is again the criterion for correct convergence applied to language comprehension (Levelt and Flores d'Arcais, 1987). The problem is that if, for example, the word *guitarist* is presented, all the information for the activation for the word *guitar* is available as well. How is the word *guitar* going to be excluded? In many languages it is possible to construct more complex words by adding morphemes to it (Turkish!). So there should be a principle to determine word boundaries. Levelt and Flores d'Arcais propose a maximalisation principle implying that a definite decision about a word is only made if an additional segment leads to a non-word or to a contextually inappropriate word. This requires a theory that specifies how context affects word segmentation, in particular when the words are morphologically complex. The maximalisation principle seems to reflect the same kind of process as the principle of late closure in syntactic parsing (to be discussed below) in the sense that a structure is computed by relating new incoming information to the information that has just been processed. This may be motivated by the need to reduce cognitive load.

Graphemic Decoding

The input for this process is the visual form representation of letters and letter strings. The output is the lexical information retrieved from the lexicon. There are no segmentation processes (except in reading handwriting). The processes in this subsystem consist in the identification and the recognition of words.

A central question is how words in the mental lexicon are accessed. An influential model is the dual route model (Coltheart, 1978). According to this model there are two functionally independent methods of word processing. One is direct visual access and involves lexical knowledge. The visual characteristics of a word are mapped directly onto the lexical representation in the lexicon. The other way of processing consists in the translation of the visual code into a phonological code on the basis of nonlexical grapheme-phoneme conversion rules. An alternative model for the dual route model is the analogy model (Glushko, 1979; Kay and Marcel, 1981). This model claims that, when a word is presented, words and word segments are activated that are similar to the presented word. The pronunciation of the presented word results from the synthesized activation of these segments. New words are pronounced by reference to similar words that are known. Patterson and Coltheart (1987), in a discussion of the role of phonological processes in reading, argue that the difference between dual route models and analogy models is not so radical as has been supposed. In fact, most analogy models happen to be dual process models. They accept two different print-to-sound translation procedures, one at the word level and one at the subword level. The former implies that the phonological representation of a word is looked up as a stored entity corresponding to the whole letter string; the latter implies that the phonological code is assembled from the phonological translations of subcomponents. They argue that both kinds of phonological procedures are automatically activated in silent and oral reading. Furthermore, they argue that phonological coding might not be the basis for word recognition, but might serve as a temporary record to aid comprehension.

Another question is what the units are in word recognition: words, sublexical units or letters. Examples of sublexical units are spelling patterns (Gibson, Shurcliff and Jonas, 1970) and syllables (Smith and Spoehr, 1974) that are considered as orthographic units. Research on these and other notions of orthography is discussed in Henderson, 1982. Recent research has challenged the existence of a separate level of sublexical units (Henderson, 1987). The effect of sublexical units in reading can be described in connectionist models of word recognition (McClelland and Rumelhart, 1981) in which no intervening level between letters and words is postulated. For example, Seidenberg (1987) argues that syllables are not represented as such in the word recognition process. The effect of syllables and other sublexical structures derives from orthographic redundancy, which can be explained in terms of the distribution of letters in the lexicon.

Syntactic Parsing

The input to the parser are the word forms that have been identified in the previous process. The output is the syntactic structure assigned to the words in the sentence. The question is how this structure is assigned. An important topic for research is the relation between linguistic theories of parsing and psycholinguistic theories of sentence processing. The question is whether these parsers can serve as a model for human sentence processing.

Early research on sentence processing has produced a number of syntactic strategies by which a sentence is segmented into constituents (Fodor and Garrett, 1967). The occurrence of a relative pronoun, for example, may facilitate the segmentation of a sentence into a main and a subordinate clause. Fodor and Garrett also proposed stategies the reader may use to deduce deep structure relations from surface characteristics of the sentences. Bever (1970) formulated a number of non-transformational strategies for parsing. For example, in any sentence the first clause with a noun-verb-(noun) sequence is interpreted as the main clause, unless it is marked as a subordinate by a subordinate conjunction. Similarly, Kimball (1973) proposed a set of principles for surface parsing. According to Frazier, many of these stategies can be considered as instances of two stategies: minimal attachment and late closure. (Frazier and Fodor, 1978; Frazier, 1987). The minimal attachment strategy implies that the perceiver postulates the minimal number of nodes in parsing a sentence. This strategy can be illustrated by the sentence: *The girl knew the answer by heart* in contrast to *The girl knew the answer was correct.* In the second sentence the initially assigned structure has to be changed by adding an S node. The other strategy is late closure: assign new items to the clause or phrase currently being processed, if grammatically permissible. late closure leads to interpreting *a mile* as direct object in the following sentences: *Since Jay always jogs a mile this seems like a short distance to him. Since Jay always jogs a mile seems like a short distance to him.* The predictions based on these principles are confirmed in experiments (Frazier and Rayner, 1982). For example, the eyes fixated the words *was correct* in the sentence given above longer than in a control sentence. This suggests that the syntactic parsing is accomplished immediately (for possible counterevidence see Crain and Steedman, 1985, and below). The minimal attachment and late closure principles serve to minimize the memory load in sentence processing. The effect is that the structuring of the current information is not delayed. In that sense these principles are similar to the immediacy principle of Just and Carpenter (1980). These principles may very well be universal principles in language processing.

Semantic Analysis

The input for the semantic analysis are the word meanings retrieved from the mental lexicon, and, presumably, the syntactic structure of the sentence derived from the syntactic processor. The output of the semantic analyser is a representation of the conceptual relations among the elements in the sentence.

It is not quite clear whether the syntactic structure is indeed part of the input for the semantic processor. It is conceivable that the semantic analysis contributes to the computation of the structure of the sentence. The problem of the (in)dependence of these two processors has not been solved. Some positions will be discussed later.

A second question is the demarcation between the semantic processor and the message interpreter. It makes sense to distinguish between mental model and semantic represent ation. A differentiation is frequently made in the following way. The output of the semantic processor is the representation of the meaning of the sentence independently of its verbal and pragmatic context. At the message level, the sentences are interpreted in relation to the other sentences in the discourse and in relation to the discourse context. The distinction is debatable, however. It is very likely that the semantic processes use contextual information. It is certainly not always the case that a literal meaning of a sentence is computed before the intended meaning is derived.

Models that have been proposed for sentence representation, like those for knowledge representation in general, are in particular network models and propositional models (these two do not necessarily exclude each other). The process of "concatenating" word meanings so as to form a conceptual representation of the sentence, may be conceived of as an activation process in a network (which may be the network of a particular schema) or as a process of connecting propositions that share arguments or that are connected by anaphoric relations. But how that process takes place is still ill understood. There is some evidence for the use of semantic strategies: on the basis of particular words in the sentence, the language understander identifies the semantic roles of the elements mentioned in the sentence and derives a representation (Clark and Clark, 1977; Just and Carpenter, 1987). This approach is compatible with a procedural conception of meaning: the meaning of a word is considered as a procedure that has to be applied to its context.

Relations between Subsystems

Just as in the case of language production, the question should be asked what the relations are between the subsystems. How are the processes coordinated and how are the various kinds of information integrated in understanding language? Some research will be presented that deals with the question whether the lexical processes and the syntactic processes in language understanding are autonomous. No conclusive answers are available yet.

Lexical Processes.   The question is whether syntactic and semantic information in the sentence affects the course of the lexical processes. Evidence for an interaction between lexical processes and syntactic/semantic processes was obtained by Morton and Long (1976) who found that word recognition is speeded up by the sentence context. A phoneme in a word that occurs in a plausible context is recognized more quickly than a phoneme in a word that occurs in an implausible context. Other evidence for the interaction between lexical processes and sentence level processes has been obtained by Marslen-Wilson (1987), and Brown, Marslen-Wilson and Tyler (ms.) who showed that a spoken word in context can be recognized at a moment when not enough information is available yet to uniquely identify that word on the basis of its acoustic information alone. The effect of several kinds of context on word recognition was demonstrated.

Evidence for autonomous lexical processes, on the other hand, has been obtained by Swinney (1979). He found that both meanings of an ambiguous word were initially activated. Only after about 200 msec did the process converge on the contextually appropriate word. This supports the idea that the context does not affect the initial lexical process, but selects among several autonomously activated word meanings (Norris, 1982). Forster (1979) maintains the autonomy hypothesis by claiming that it is not the lexical access that is speeded up by the context, but a decision process in a general problem solver.

Syntactic Processes.   The same questions have been investigated with respect to syntactic processing. Frazier (1987) reviews a lot of the literature concerning the question whether lexical and thematic (world knowledge) information influence the syntactic processor. On the one hand it has been argued (Ford, Bresnan and Kaplan, 1983) that lexical preferences influence syntactic processes. Since *want* in general has one argument in its complement and *position* two, the preferred analyses for the following sentences differ:

The woman positioned [the dress] on that rack
The woman wanted [the dress on that rack]

That was what they did indeed find (see also the lexical strategies of Fodor, Garrett and Bever, 1968). Frazier claims, however, that the results do not exclude the possibility that lexical preferences do not guide the initial syntactic parsing, but are used later to filter or to evaluate particular analyses that have been produced autonomously. Results of Mitchell (1987) support the autonomy hypothesis. Since *departed* is an obligatorily intransitive verb, readers making use of this lexical information would have no problem with the sentence *After the audience had departed the actors sat down for a well-deserved drink*. They would analyse that sentence correctly right away. It appeared, however, that initially the incorrect transitive analysis was taken

The other question is whether syntactic processing depends on thematic information from the context. Tyler and Marslen-Wilson (1977) demonstrated that listeners use contextual information for the on-line solution of a syntactic ambiguity. However, the non-interaction interpretation implying that initially two readings are computed, one of which is selected by the context, is hard to exclude.

Crain and Steedman (1985) argue similarly that parsing is affected by discourse factors. They propose a number of strategies that guarantee a maximally compatible and plausible reading for a sentence in a given context. If plausibility affects parsing, one would predict that the sentence *The teachers taught by the Berlitz method passed the test* is more frequently judged as ungrammatical than the sentence in which *teachers* is replaced by *children*, since teachers are more plausible subjects of *taught* than children. This was indeed found.

Strong evidence for the autonomy hypothesis, on the other hand, was obtained by Ferreira and Clifton (1986) and by Rayner, Carlson and Frazier (1983). Rayner et al. registered eye movements for the sentences:

The florist sent the flowers was very pleased
The performer sent the flowers was very pleased

Although the relative clause interpretation of *sent the flowers* is much more likely in the performer sentence than in the florist sentence, the pattern of regressive eye movements from *was pleased* to *performer sent* was similar to the regressions from *was pleased* to *florist sent*. Rayner et al. suggest that syntactic and thematic processes occur in parallel, but that the thematic information does not govern the selection of the initial syntactic analysis.

Lexicon

The lexicon is the central store of information concerning words. It contains multiple sources of information, in particular information about the form of words (phonological, morphological, orthographic and articulatory properties), about their syntactic functions and their meanings. These kinds of information are used by the different processors in the system.

Many aspects of the lexicon are still ill-understood, both as to its structure and as to the processes involved in accessing the lexicon in language production and comprehension. One of the problems (how the processes in production and comprehension converge on the selection of the correct word) has been mentioned already. Only a few other questions will be reviewed here.

One aspect a theory of the lexicon should account for is the interconnectedness of the lexicon. The lexicon may be entered in different ways, for example through sounds and shapes in comprehension, and through meaning or even through syntax in production. But in all cases the information that in principle becomes available is the complete information stored in the lexicon.

morphological structure and access of morphologically complex words are important topics of research. A central question is whether complex words are stored as separate entities or whether only stems are stored and complex words are derived by a rule system. There is evidence that the answers to these questions are different for different languages (Jarvella, Job, Sandstrom and Schreuder, 1987). If a language has many inflected forms, it is less likely that all the complex words are stored separately than when a language has a simple inflectional system. There seems to be a trade-off between computation and storage. As far as word access is concerned, morphologically complex words are not more difficult to process than monomorphematic words. Morphologically complex words do not have to be retrieved by accessing their stem (Cutler, 1983).

The representation of word meanings is an issue that has been investigated for some time in psycholinguistics. Several kinds of representation are proposed for word meanings: features, networks, meaning postulates, prototypes, procedures. The development of procedural semantics is an important development in language research. Word meanings are considered as instructions to perform certain procedures in order to construct the representation of the sentence. The kind of procedure is indicated by the lexical item. For example, the procedure for understanding a definite noun phrase can be considered as a search for a particular entity in the memory store and to predicate the new information in the sentence to that entity (Haviland and Clark, 1974); the procedure for understanding spatial relations may be the execution of a kind of spatial calculation (Johnson-Laird, 1983). A procedural representation of word meanings is very important for language technological applications (e.g. machine translation).

A further question is to what extent there are different lexicons for the different modalities in language behavior (visual and auditory production and comprehension) or whether there is a single list of lexical elements that is accessed differently in speaking, writing, reading and listening. Evidence for different access routes has been obtained by Marshall and Newcombe (1973) who defined particular syndromes of reading disorders (in particular surface dyslexica anddeep dyslexia) in terms of particular breakdowns in an information processing model for normal reading (see also Coltheart, Patterson and Marshall, 1980, and Patterson, Marshall and Coltheart, 1985). Deep dyslexic patients are unable to read non-words and they make semantic errors; for example they read *turtle* as *crocodile*. This is explained by assuming that the access to the lexicon in these patients is meaning-based. The question then is whether the semantic errors that are made are due to the loss of specific semantic distinctions or to the impossibility to retrieve the correct names. According to Coltheart (1987b) there is no single explanation that applies to all deep dyslexic patients. Surface dyslexics on the other hand read words by sounding out the letters and make errors by pronouncing irregular words as if they were regular. The access to the lexicon is by letter-sound conversion. The question now is whether the irregular words are not accessed at all or whether these words cannot be produced at an output stage. Again, there seems to be no single explanation for all deep dyslexic patients.

Actually, since Marshall and Newcombe (1973) an increasing number of studies has been conducted on language disorders of (brain damaged) patients that are very relevant for lexical processes. In this research patients are requested to perform specific production or comprehension tasks in oral or written language, the execution of which requires particular linguistic knowledge. On the basis of the analysis of patients' performance one tries to identify the input and output subsystems of the lexicon and the relations between them. Some of the current controversies are discussed by Coltheart (1987b): is there a single phonological lexicon that is used both for understanding and for producing words or are there separate input and output lexicons? Is there a single orthographic lexicon for understanding and producing words? Is there a single semantic lexicon or is there a separate verbal and visual semantic lexicon?

World Knowledge

The second knowledge store used in the language processing system is knowledge about the world including the discourse context. The discourse context includes the previous discourse and the intentions of the discourse participants. Psycholinguistic research has to account for the way in which conceptual information and intentions influence the structure of utterances. For example, if, according to some previously discussed theories, conceptual accessibility influences the syntactic forms of the sentences produced, and thematic information affects syntactic decisions in parsing, then the question is how these dependencies have to be accounted for. Similarly, if one has to account for the way in which cues in a text activate conceptual information, one has to have a theory about knowledge representation and about the interaction between knowledge and language. Carlson and Tanenhaus (1987) suggest that thematic roles provide a mechanism for the interaction between syntactic processing, discourse model and world knowledge. It is essential for the study of language processes that more insight should be obtained into knowledge representation and human intentionality. These topics are beyond the scope of this paper.

PSYCHOLINGUISTIC RESEARCH IN A MULTI-LANGUAGE CONTEXT

Psycholinguistics aims at a theory of language production, comprehension and acquisition. The theory must specify how language behavior is determined by properties of the information processing system and by properties of the specific language. Therefore, it is imperative that psycholinguists conduct their research in several languages. A theory of English processing is not a theory of language processing. A much more articulated theory of language behavior will be obtained and unjustified generalizations will be avoided, if language behavior is studied in several languages. The European situation offers very good opportunities for cross-linguistic research.

With respect to sentence processing, one may ask whether there are universal parsing strategies. Since the minimal attachment and the late closure principles lead to a rapid structuring of the information and to a decrease of processing load, they are good candidates for universal principles. That theory was contrasted with theories that imply that the initial syntactic analysis depends on lexical preferences. Frazier (1987) argues that if the latter theory is correct, one would expect parsing difficulties in head (verb) final phrases, since the lexical information is then available only when the verb is processed. Frazier found no evidence for such delayed parsing in languages with head-final verb phrases such as embedded phrases in Dutch. The predictions of the minimal attachment and the late closure principles were upheld. This supports the universal character of the two principles.

The study of several languages is also particularly important with respect to questions of storage versus computation in the lexicon. Languages that differ in inflections and derivations offer a good opportunity to study how morphologically complex words are stored and what the consequences are for the processes involved in accessing the information.

Similarly, issues with respect to word meanings can fruitfully be investigated cross-linguisticallly. The variety of languages represented in Europe gives researchers a good opportunity to gain insight into the variable relation between words and conceptual information and to study how conceptual information is mapped onto language. This research is particularly pertinent to (automatic) translation. Languages differ in the distinctions they make within a particular conceptual category, such as causality or conditionality. For example, the Dutch language has several words to express a causal relation. The conceptual distinctions drawn by these words do not map in a one-to-one correspondence onto English words. The distinctions between these different words should be analysed in terms of underlying concepts or dimensions. Such an analysis will give insight into the categories underlying these words, and into the conceptual relations between the words. A specification of word meanings in terms of underlying concepts can be used in programming language production and understanding. The underlying concepts are then treated as conditions to be tested for the selection of a particular word or for the verification of a particular interpretation. The comparison of different languages also offers a very useful way to test theories. The theory, preferably implemented in a translation program, should be able to specify the rules for choosing the correct interpretation of a word and to translate it correctly into the other language.

Another issue is the distinction between preconditions and satisfaction conditions of predicates (Seuren, 1985). Satisfaction conditions generate entailments; preconditions generate presuppositions. For example, the satisfaction condition for the word *bald* is the absence of what is normally present. The preconditions specify which surfaces can be bald. If the satisfaction conditions of a predicate are not fulfilled, the expression is false. If the preconditions are not fulfilled, lexical inappropriateness results. Languages seem to differ substantially in the preconditions of lexical items. For example, the Dutch word *kaal* ("bald") can be attributed to humans and non-humans, as its English equivalent, but also to other entities such as landscapes. This distinction offers a fruitful means for the description of semantic structures. It will also be of great value in applications, such as dictionaries and translation machines.

Differences between languages with respect to the mapping between conceptual information and language occur not only at the word level, but also at the sentence or discourse level. Languages differ with respect to the ways in which discourse functions are expressed, e.g. by means of discourse markers or by means of particles. Again, research into these aspects of the discourse will be very helpful in translation programs.

The cross-linguistic study of language acquisition may increase our understanding of how the conceptual resources that are presumably common to all human beings are put to use in discovering the semantic classification system characteristic of the different languages.

PSYCHOLINGUISTICS AND LANGUAGE TECHNOLOGY

Research on the topics that have been discussed in the previous section will greatly increase our understanding of fundamental issues in language production and comprehension. At the same time, a better understanding of the ways in which we use language is a prerequisite for the development of applications. An important issue in the coming years will be the improvement of communication in natural language between man and machines. Technological applications for which research in psycholinguistics will be required include natural language interfaces, machine assisted translation, and text processing.

Natural Language Interface

An increasing number of people will have to interact in the near future with information processing systems. Hence it is very important to make these systems more accessible by developing user-friendly interfaces. Dialogue systems will be developed in the future that are increasingly flexible, in the sense that they are not only able to give answers that are stored, but also to derive the answers from the system's knowledge. Therefore, these systems should be intelligent, knowledge-based interfaces that have an internal representation of the data base, an interpretation of the questions that are asked and an interpretation (model) of the user. By this last requirement is meant that the system has information about pragmatic aspects of the dialogue, and about the intentions, expectations and knowledge of the user. On the basis of these representations the system will be able to infer what information it should provide, how this should be formulated, and what information can be left implicit.

Systems of this sort can be developed only if they are highly restricted with respect to the knowledge domain. A characteristic of human interlocutors is that they are not restricted at all and may provide all kinds of apparently irrelevant information. It is only by having a large amount of knowledge that the relevance of the utterances of a human interlocutor for the topic of the conversation can be determined, but the implementation of a full-scale general knowledge base is not to be expected in the near future. All that can be hoped for is for knowledge in limited domains to be represented. The system should be able to find out whether an utterance is related to the topic of the conversation at all and to determine what information is desired. The way in which this can be achieved is by having the system ask questions so as to find out how the utterances of the interlocutor relate to the domain that is under discussion.

Machine Translation

Translation means processing the lexical, syntactic, semantic and pragmatic information so as to extract the interpretation of a message in a source language, and to express it in a target language. This requires a thorough understanding of the source and target language, as well as an understanding of the mapping of language onto knowledge representations and vice versa. An important issue in translation is how such an interpretation of a message should be represented in an intermediary representation system (if such a system is preferred to a direct translation system that does not have an intermediary representation) and what the nature of that representation system should be in order to obtain the best possible system. What would work best: one universal intermediary representation system (interlingua approach) or representation systems which depend on the two languages (transfer approach)? In the latter case there may be several intermediary representations in the translation from one language into another. So, automatic translation by interlingua and transfer systems necessitates the study of representation systems onto which the source language is mapped and from which the target language is produced. Translation requires an understanding of differences between the languages with respect to the ways in which information is expressed in language. This applies to words (meanings that can be expressed in one word in a particular language may not be expressible by a single word of the other language), but also to phenomena at the sentence and discourse level. Languages may differ, for example, in their use of rhetorical devices: English uses quite a lot of discourse markers, whereas German and Dutch use many particles to express similar functions.

A serious problem for automatic translation is that a translation is only possible if a large amount of knowledge is implemented. Therefore, research on knowledge representation is crucial

The development of computer-based dictionaries is a very important requirement for all technological applications. The dictionary should contain information about phonological, orthographic, morphological, articulatory, syntactic and semantic properties of the lexical items and procedures for accessing the information.

Automatic Text Processing

Important technological achievements are to be expected in automatic text processing, both in text analysis and text generation. However, research on human comprehension and production of language is necessary to make these developments possible.

A future objective is to have a system that can read a text, in the sense that it is able to process the text and to communicate to human users what they want to know about it, for example to give a summary. Some initial systems have already achieved results in the applied area. A simple method is the identification in a text of prespecified key words. This requires a fair amount of linguistic knowledge concerning word forms, in particular about the morphology and syntax of words. In this way, the location of relevant content in a text can be determined.

A more complex process requires the system itself to analyse the text to extract its meaning. A lot of research is currently being conducted on the organisation and structure of connected sentences. Rules are being developed for the identification of the topic in a particular passage, for determining what information is foregrounded and what is backgrounded, and for analyzing the organisation of the text in such a way that the relative importance of the units it contains can be determined. These rules, derived from the analysis of natural texts as well as from research on human discourse processing, can (and have been) implemented and will greatly increase the power of automatic text analysis systems. Again, progress in this direction depends very much on restricting the knowledge domain. More particularly, it is not to be expected that the identification of the main points in a text can be based purely on text-structural properties and linguistic knowledge; text analysis also requires a knowledge representation of the domain.

Text analysis systems will also be able to identify and correct errors, not only spelling errors, but also more complex errors such as grammatical errors, redundancies, and inconsistencies. Error identification will depend on the (syntactic and semantic) knowledge incorporated in the system.

Important applications will also be realized in text generation. Current text generators produce stereotypical texts from a conceptual representation. It is unrealistic to suppose that fully acceptable and fluent text generators will be manufactured within ten to fifteen years. But much progress can be made in the generation of texts within specific contexts, e.g. as output from expert systems. Systems will become more flexible and powerful to the extent that more knowledge about the domain and more linguistic knowledge can be implemented.

In conclusion, the technological applications require routines for all the language processes, such as word recognition, contextual disambiguation, parsing, semantic interpretation and interpretation at the discourse level. A better understanding of human language processing will be instrumental in the development of these applications.

ACKNOWLEDGEMENTS

Discussions with the following persons on a previous version of this paper are gratefully acknowledged: David Bree, Pim Levelt, Wietske Vonk, Lyn Frazier, Gerard Kempen, Rob Schreuder, Harry Bunt, Melissa Bowerman, Gisela Redeker, Anne Cutler, Raymond van Rijnsoever, and Alan Garnham. A number of corrections of English were made by Pieter Nieuwint.

REFERENCES

Bever, T.G. (1970). The cognitive basis for linguistic structures. In J.R.Hayes (Ed.), *Cognition and the development of language*. New York: Wiley.

Bock, K. (1987a). An effect of the accessibility of word forms on sentence structure. *Journal of Memory and Language, 26*, 119-137.

Bock, K. (1987b). Coordinating words and syntax in speech plans. In A.Ellis (Ed.), *Progress in the psychology of language. Vol.3*. London: Erlbaum.

Bosch, P. (1983). *Agreement and anaphora*, London: Academic Press.

Brown, C.M., Marslen-Wilson, W.D., & Tyler, L.K. *Sensory and contextual factors in spoken word recognition*. Manuscript, Max-Planck-Institut für Psycholinguistik, Nijmegen.

Carlson, G.N., & Tanenhaus, M.K. (1987) *Thematic roles and language comprehension*. Manuscript.

Clark, H.H., & Clark, E.V. (1977). *Psychology and language*. New York: Harcourt, Brace, Jovanovich.

Coltheart, M. (1978). Lexical access in simple reading tasks. In G.Underwood (Ed.), *Strategies of human information processing*. London: Academic Press.

Coltheart, M. (Ed.). (1987a). *The psychology of language*. London: Lawrence Erlbaum.

Coltheart, M. (1987b). Functional architecture of the language-processing system. In M. Coltheart, G.

Sartori, & R Job (Eds.), *The cognitive neuropsychology of language*. London: Lawrence Erlbaum.

Coltheart, M., Patterson, K., & Marshall, J.C. (Eds.).(1980). *Deep dyslexia*. London: Routledge & Kegan Paul.

Coltheart, M., Sartori, G., & Job, R. (Eds.). (1987). *The cognitive neuropsychology of language*. London: Lawrence Erlbaum.

Crain, S., & Steedman, M. (1985). On not being led up the garden-path: The use of context by the psychological parser. In D.Dowty, L.Karttunen, & A.Zwicky (Eds.), *Natural language parsing*. Cambridge: Cambridge University Press.

Cutler, A. (1983). Lexical complexity and sentence processing. In G.B. Flores d'Arcais & R.J.Jarvella (Eds.), *The process of language understanding*. London: Wiley.

Dell, G.S. (1985). Positive feedback in hierarchical connectionist models: Applications to language production. *Cognitive Science*, *9*, 3-23.

Dell, G.S. (1986). A spreading activation theory of retrieval in sentence production. *Psychological Review*, *93*, 283-321.

Dell, G.S., & Reich. P.A. (1981). Stages in sentence production: An analysis of speech error data. *Journal of Verbal Learning and Verbal Behavior*, *20*, 611-629.

Fauconnier, G. (1985). *Mental spaces: Aspects of meaning construction in natural language*. Cambridge: M.I.T.Press.

Ferreira, F., & Clifton, C. (1986). The independence of syntactic processing. *Journal of Memory and Language*, *25*, 348-368.

Fodor, J.A., & Garrett, M.F. (1967). Some syntactic determinants of sentential complexity. *Perception and Psychophysics*, *2*, 289-296.

Fodor, J.A., Garrett, M.F., & Bever, T.G. (1968). Some syntactic determinants of sentential complexity. II Verb structure. *Perception and Psychophysics*, *3*, 453-461.

Ford, M. (1982). Sentence planning units: Implications for the speaker's representation of meaningful relations underlying sentences. In J.W.Bresnan (Ed.), *The mental representation of grammatical relations*. Cambridge: M.I.T.Press.

Ford, M., Bresnan, J.,& Kaplan, R. (1983). A competence-based theory of syntactic closure. In J.Bresnan (Ed.), *The mental representation of grammatical relations*. Cambridge: M.I.T.Press.

Ford, M., & Holmes, V.M. (1978). Planning units and syntax in sentence production. *Cognition*, *6*, 35-53.

Forster, K.I. (1976). Accessing the mental lexicon. In R.J.Wales & E.C.T.Walker (Eds.), *New approaches to language mechanisms*. Amsterdam: North Holland.

Forster, K.I. (1979). Levels of processing and the structure of the language processor. In W.E.Cooper & E.C.T.Walker (Eds.), *Sentence processing: Psycholinguistic studies presented to Merrill Garrett*. Hillsdale: Lawrence Erlbaum.

Frazier, L. (1987). Sentence processing: a tutorial review. In M.Coltheart (Ed.), *The psychology of reading. London: Lawrence Erlbaum*.

Frazier, L., & Fodor, J.D. (1978). The sausage machine: a new two-stage parsing model. *Cognition*, *6*, 291-325.

Frazier, L., & Rayner, K. (1982). Making and correcting errors during sentence comprehension: Eye movements in analysis of structurally ambiguous sentences. *Cognitive Psychology*, *14*, 178-210.

Garnham, A. (1985). *Psycholinguistics: central topics*. London: Methuen.

Garnham, A. (1987a). Understanding anaphora. In A.W.Ellis (Ed.), *Progress in the psychology of language, vol. 3*. London: Lawrence Erlbaum.

Garnham, A. (1987b). *Mental models as representation of discourse and text*. Chichester: Ellis Horwood.

Garrett, M.F. (1975). The analysis of sentence production. In G.H.Bower (Ed.), *The psychology of learning and motivation, Vol. 9*. New York: Academic Press.

Garrett, M.F. (1980). Levels of processing in sentence production. In B. Butterworth (Ed.), *Language production. Vol. 1: speech and talk*. New York: Academic Press.

Garrett, M.F. (1982). Production of speech: Observations from normal and pathological language use.

In : A. Ellis (Ed.), *Normality and pathology in cognitive functions.* London: Academic Press.

Gibson, E.J., Shurcliff, A., & Jonas, A. (1970). Utilization of spelling patterns by deaf and hearing subjects. In H.Levin & J.P.Williams (Eds.), *Basic studies on reading.* New York: Basic Books.

Glushko, R. (1979). The organization and activation of orthographic knowledge in reading aloud. *Journal of Experimental Psychology: Human Perception & Performance, 5,* 674-691.

Grosjean, F., Grosjean, L., & Lane, H. (1979). The patterns of silence: Performance structures in sentence production. *Cognitive Psychology, 11,* 58-81.

Grosz, B.J., & Sidner, C.L. (1986). Attention, intentions, and the structure of discourse. *Computational Linguistics, 12,* 175-204.

Haviland, S.E., & Clark, H.H. (1974). What's new? Acquiring new information as a process of understanding. *Journal of Verbal Learning and Verbal Behavior, 13,* 512-521.

Henderson, L. (1987). Word recognition: A tutorial view. In M.Coltheart (Ed.), *The psychology of reading,* London: Lawrence Erlbaum.

Jarvella, R.J., Job, R., Sandstrom, G. & Schreuder, R. (1987). Morphological constraints on word recognition. In A.Allport, D.Mackay, W.Prinz & E.Scheerer (Eds.), *Language production and perception.* London: Academic Press.

Johnson-Laird, P.N. (1983). *Mental models.* Cambridge: Cambridge University Press.

Just, M.A. & Carpenter, P.A. (1980). A theory of reading: From eye fixations to comprehension. *Psychological Review, 87,* 329-354.

Just, M.A. & Carpenter, P.A. (1987). *The psychology of reading and comprehension.* Boston: Allyn and Bacon.

Kamp, H. (1981). A theory of truth and semantic representation. In J.A.G.Groenendijk, T.M.V.Janssen & M.B.J.Stokhof (Eds.), *Formal methods in the study of language.* Amsterdam: Mathematisch Centrum.

Kay, J. & Marcel, A. (1981). One process, not two, in reading words aloud: Lexical analogies do the work of non-lexical rules. *Quarterly Journal of Experimental Psychology, 33A,* 397-413.

Kempen, G. & Hoenkamp, E. (1987). An incremental procedural grammar for sentence formulation. *Cognitive Science, 11,* 201-258.

Kimball, J. (1973). Seven principles of surface structure parsing in natural language. *Cognition, 2,* 15-47.

Levelt, W.J.M. (1981). The speaker's linearization problem. *Philosophical Transactions of the Royal Society London* B295, 305-315.

Levelt, W.J.M. (1983). Monitoring and self-repair in speech. *Cognition, 14,* 41-104.

Levelt, W.J.M. (1989). *Speaking: From intention to articulation.* Cambridge: MIT Press.

Levelt, W.J.M. & Flores d'Arcais, G.B. (1987). *Snelheid en uniciteit bij lexicale toegang.* In H.F.M. Crombach, L.J.Th. van der Kamp & C.A.J. Vlek (Eds.), *De psychologie voorbij. Ontwikkelingen rond model, metriek en methode in de gedragswetenschappen.* Lisse: Swets & Zeitlinger.

Levelt, W.J.M. & Maassen, B. (1981). Lexical search and order of mention in sentence production. In W.Klein & W.J.M.Levelt (Eds.), *Crossing the boundaries in linguistics.* Dordrecht: Reidel.

Maclay, H & Osgood, C.E. (1959). Hesitation phenomena in spontaneous English speech. *Word, 15,* 19-44.

Marr, D. (1982). *Vision.* San Francisco: Freeman.

Marshall, J.C., & Newcombe, F. (1973). Patterns of paralexia. *Journal of Psycholinguistic Research, 2,* 175-199.

Marslen-Wilson, W.D. (1987). Functional parallelism in spoken word recognition. *Cognition, 25,* 71-102.

Marslen-Wilson, W.D. & Welsh, A. (1978). Processing interactions and lexical access during word recognition in continuous speech. *Cognitive Psychology, 10,* 29-63.

McClelland, J.L., & Rumelhart, D.M. (1981). An interactive-activation model of context effects in letter perception. *Psychological Review, 88,* 375-407.

Mitchell, D.C. (1987). Lexical guidance in human parsing: Locus and processing characteristics. In M.Coltheart (Ed.), *The psychology of reading.* London: Lawrence Erlbaum.

Morton, J. (1969). Interaction of information in word *recognition*. Psychological Review, *76*, 165-178.

Morton, J. & Long, J. (1976). Effect of word transition probability on phoneme identification. *Journal of Verbal Learning and Verbal Behavior*, *15*, 43-51.

Noordman, L.G.M. & Vonk, W. (1987) Knowledge acquisition through text processing In J.Engelkamp, K.Lorenz, & B.Sandig (Eds.), *Wissensrepräsentation und Wissensaustausch*. St. Ingbert: Röhrig.

Norris, D.G. (1982). Autonomous processes in comprehension: A reply to Marslen-Wilson and Tyler. *Cognition*, *11*, 97-101.

Patterson, K., & Coltheart, V. (1987). Phonological processes in reading: A tutorial review. In M.Coltheart (Ed.), *The psychology of reading*. London: Lawrence Erlbaum.

Patterson, K., Marshall, J.C., & Coltheart, M. (Eds.). (1985). *Surface dyslexia: Cognitive and neuropsychological studies of phonological reading*. London: Lawrence Erlbaum.

Rayner, K., Carlson, M., & Frazier, L. (1983). The interaction of syntax and semantics during sentence processing: Eye movements in the analysis of semantically biased sentences. *Journal of Verbal Learning and Verbal Behavior*, *22*, 358-374.

Riesbeck, C.K. (1982). Realistic language comprehension. In W.G.Lehnert & M.H.Ringle (Eds.), *Strategies for natural language processing*. Hillsdale: Lawrence Erlbaum.

Sanford, A.J. & Garrod, S.C. (1981). *Understanding written language: Explorations in comprehension beyond the sentence*. Chichester: Wiley.

Seidenberg, M.S. (1987). Sublexical structures in visual word recognition: Access units or orthographic redundancy? In M.Coltheart (Ed.), *The psychology of reading*, London: Lawrence Erlbaum.

Seuren, P.A.M. (1985). *Discourse semantics*. Oxford: Basil Blackwell.

Sidner, C.L. (1983). Focusing and discourse. *Discourse Processes*, *6*, 107-130.

Smith, E.E., & Spoehr, K.T. (1974). The perception of printed English: A theoretical perspective. In B.H.Kantowitz (Ed.), *Human information processing: Tutorials in performance and cognition*. Potomac: Lawrence Erlbaum.

Stemberger, J.P. (1985). An interactive model of language production. In A.W.Ellis (Ed.), *Progress in the psychology of language, vol. 1*, London: Lawrence Erlbaum.

Swinney, D.A. (1979). Lexical access during sentence comprehension: (Re)considerations of context effects. *Journal of Verbal Learning and Verbal Behavior*, *18*, 545-569.

Tyler, L.K. & Marslen-Wilson, W.D. (1977). The on-line effects of semantic context on syntactic processing. *Journal of Verbal Learning and Verbal Behavior*, *16*, 683-692.

Vonk, W. (1985). The immediacy of inferences in the understanding of pronouns. In G.Rickheit & H.Strohner (Eds.), *Inferences in text processing*. Amsterdam: North Holland.

Wijk, C. van & Kempen, G. (1982). Kost zinsbouw echt tijd? In R.Stuip & W.Zwanenburg (Eds.), *Handelingen van het 37ste Nederlands Filologencongres*. Amsterdam: Holland Universiteits Pers.

Wijk, C. van, & Kempen, G. (1987). A dual system for producing self-repairs in spontaneous speech: Evidence from experimentally elicited corrections. *Cognitive Psychology*, *19*, 403-440.

Yngve, V.H. (1960). A model and an hypothesis for language structure. *Proceedings of the American Philosophical Society*, *104*, 444-466.

CHAPTER 7

Experimentation and Computation in Cognitive Science

John Fox

Imperial Cancer Research Fund Laboratories,
London , England

The relative contributions to psychology of computational studies and experimental enquiries are considered in the light of recent events in artificial intelligence and cognitive science. Some old criticisms of psychology's overdependence on experimental methodology are recalled, though doubts about the scientific status of computational studies in isolation are acknowledged. The primary theme of the paper is the need for experimental investigations *in combination with* computational studies, while being informed by the requirements of, and behaviour on, tasks of realistic complexity. It argues that the recent commercialisation of AI has weakened an important line of scientific enquiry, that theories expressed in symbolic, computational terms are still needed, and that connectionist concepts are not an adequate substitute.

INTRODUCTION

This is a commentary on what cognitive science is, or rather what it seems to be trying to do and how it is trying to do it. It reflects a concern that serious theoretical and methodological difficulties in experimental cognitive psychology, which have been under discussion for a decade and for which at least partial solutions exist, have had so little impact on what research psychologists actually do. My concerns have become greater with the growth of significant new influences; the pressure towards artificial intelligence (AI) and the growth of connectionism in psychology.

Cognitive science was originally conceived as an area of common interest of cognitive psychology, artificial intelligence (AI) and, perhaps to lesser extents, linguistics, neurophysiology, and parts of philosophy like epistemology and logic. It was not simply a sophistication of psychology. As Norman put it in his foundational paper *What is cognitive science?* (1981)

> As a psychologist I want to understand the mechanisms of mind—the human mind. As a cognitive scientist, my goal is somewhat different. Here I no longer restrict myself to the study of the human. Now, my goal is to understand cognition in the general and in the abstract. For this purpose, I care not whether the cognition is of something natural or artificial ... How can I understand human cognition until I understand the range of cognitive mechanisms and functions?

Norman took it for granted that the field is about *discovery*, revealing general features of and constraints on flexible cognition and employing scientific disciplines. It is not about invention, the design of systems which are only constrained by the requirements of an engineering problem.

The Roots of Cognitive Science

Neisser's book *Cognitive Psychology*, published in 1967, was probably the first to give AI intelligibility and prominence in psychology. At that time the AI community was tiny and diverse, but was beginning to see itself as a sort of theoretical psychology which complemented the experimental tradition of most cognitive research. Over the next few years AI became very visible to cognitive psychologists, and progressively developed a position which was critical of the adequacy of traditional experimental methodology.

By the early seventies it had become quite aggressive, with some, though certainly not all prominent workers advocating computational theory and openly contemptuous of the efforts of experimentalists; claiming that computational work on vision, language, problem solving etc is the only serious way to proceed towards a sound theoretical foundation for understanding cognitive processes. Indeed the slogan "an AI program IS a psychological theory" was popular for a time.

This attitude of parts of the early AI community was counterproductive. It was also unconvincing to most of its targets. While strong claims were being made about the scientific significance of AI one saw inclinations in its practitioners to adopt overstrong or simplistic interpretations of psychological findings; to disregard the possible implications of arbitrary design decisions in programs which were claimed to have psychological validity, and even a lack of concern with obvious violations of firm empirical observations—indeed one suspected some lack of interest in data collection altogether. Objections, one often noticed, were waved away as "second order", "implementation details" and the like.

Cognitive Science as an Experimental Discipline

Fears that experimental psychology was over-preoccupied with the careful collection of data at the cost of effective theoretical development were not of course new. Most of us have heard, even made, comments to the effect that the subject tries too hard to be "like physics". Although AI established itself as a significant influence on psychological thinking during its vigorous early period it did not have anything like the same effect on the way psychological research was conducted. Whether the critics were too heavy handed, or whether they just failed to offer a credible alternative, cognitive psychology continued to be dominated by experimental, laboratory-oriented disciplines.

The excesses of some critics should not, however, obscure the validity of some of the criticisms—more effective critics were to be found. It may be profitable to recall two, Allen Newell and Ulric Neisser, whose criticisms have a new force in the present context.

Neisser's criticism in 1976 represented a major change, indeed disillusionment, with his position in the influential volume that more or less defined cognitive psychology a decade earlier. Neisser had come to believe, as have many others, that well intentioned efforts to achieve experimental tractability in laboratory environments results only in scientific illusions; a superficial understanding of trivial situations and tasks which are simply unrepresentative of everyday reality.

> There is still no account of how people act in or interact with the ordinary world. Indeed the assumptions that underlie most contemporary work on information processing are surprisingly like those of nineteenth-century introspective psychology, though without introspection itself. ... Lacking in ecological validity, indifferent to culture, even missing some of the main features of perception and memory as they occur in ordinary life, such a psychology could become a narrow and uninteresting specialised field.

Newell's paper *You can't play twenty questions with nature and win* (1973a) was very clear:

> Suppose that in the next thirty years we continue as we are now going. Another hundred phenomena, give or take a few dozen, will have been discovered and explored. Another forty oppositions will have been posited and resolution initiated. Will it provide the kind of encompassing of its subject matter—the behaviour of man—that we all posit as a characteristic of a mature science?

He was saying in effect that psychology is *not* like physics, or rather since this is a caricature of modern physics, it is not like eighteenth century physics. Experiments, Newell believes, have their proper place in psychology as in any natural science, but as the sole foundation for generating and evaluating complete processing models of cognition they are inadequate. His work over twenty years has continued to reflect this outlook, culminating in the development of a broad theory of general intelligence expressed in the computer program SOAR (Laird, Newell and Rosenbloom, 1987) about which more will be said later.

There are other well known grounds for worrying that an experimental science without a strong theoretical wing is vulnerable to becoming a pseudo-science. At risk of going over tediously familiar ground:

> Experiments alone do not prescribe the next set of good experiments, only interpretations of those experiments do that.
>
> Language is a poor instrument for formulating unambiguous interpretations of experiments.
>
> Disciplines which rely solely upon language are often strikingly subject to fashions, or paradigms. These can provide a sense of activity at the time but, in retrospect, cumulative progress may be hard to discern.

Newell's proposed solution for creating a strong, cumulative theoretical framework for cognitive science, and to which he has remained faithful, is to use rule based techniques (production systems) to model the behaviour of individuals on significant complex tasks. The rule-based approach supports incremental construction of formal, but modular and intelligible models. Tools can be standardised, permitting public scrutiny of the models.

Newell's views attracted, and still do attract, attention - but not so much action. Some years ago, for example, I was involved in organising a meeting on "production systems in Psychology" which was attended by about a hundred or so UK researchers. Among the conclusions the meeting came to were: cognitive modelling in general is a good thing; rule based systems in particular are an important technique, and that the community urgently needed portable, flexible software so that modelling tools could be easily accessible to researchers and students. Seven years later the software that group hoped for has not appeared and the kind of modelling that they thought was important has not noticeably increased. Indeed it may well have declined as we shall see in a moment.

There is still only a handful of significant psychology research centres where both experimental and computational studies are pursued together. As in other things Ulric Neisser himself put his finger on the problem which has continued to plague this aspect of cognitive science:

> Most of the resistance to computer modeling is passive; psychologists simply continue to make theories of other kinds, (Neisser, 1976).

The Recent Development of AI: Science or Engineering?

Originally AI seemed to fit well into Norman's definition of cognitive science, as figure 1 shows. It now seems that his assumptions about the relationship between cognitive science and AI were less straightforward than we thought. The AI community was always ambivalent about its aspirations and scientific role. Notwithstanding its considerable contributions to computer science, AI's efforts in psychology have tended to show a preference for the quick win over the march (or plod) of science. The traditions which tend to lead it away from a systematic, incremental (and admittedly sometimes boring) methodology of psychological investigation have become particularly evident since 1982, which saw publication of the famous Japanese report on Fifth Generation Computer Systems. Since then any claim that AI is as much a science as it is an engineering discipline has become even more ambiguous.

The 5G report, which promised truly "intelligent" computers for the 1990s, having linguistic, perceptual, intellectual and learning capabilities, triggered an explosion of commercial interest in AI. This was reflected worldwide in huge national and international information technology research programmes. Theoretical and applications work in expert systems; natural language and vision systems; formal foundations of computer science; new programming languages; machine architectures, and many other areas, have grown dramatically. AI has always been eclectic in its interests, now the dramatic growth in each area of interest has amounted to the establishment of a set of disciplines which are bound together by a common interest in technologies for symbolic computation, not by common interest in cognitive science (figure 1).

The availability of massive resources for research in AI systems, and the huge movement of people trained in mathematics, engineering, computer science and other disciplines (with no traditional interest in natural science) have dramatically changed what many people in the field do. The new funding might have increased basic research in cognitive science but I suspect that fundamental research in computational cognitive science may actually have declined (apart from the obvious exception of connectionism

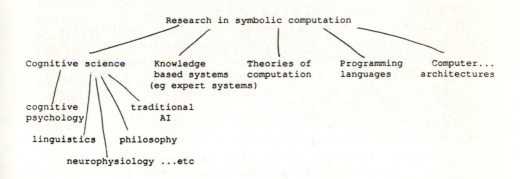

FIG. 7.1   The relationship between cognitive science and other topics which are often collectively referred to as "Artificial Intelligence". A less misleading classification is to regard this community as concerned with different aspects of symbolic computation, one of which is cognitive science. Cognitive science remains separate because of its interest in natural cognition as well as engineering.

which I shall return to shortly). The trend is reflected in the range of specialised research journals which serve AI. There are now 40 or more journals, where there used to be two or three. The two or three were quite open to papers on cognitive modelling and psychological commentary, but to my knowledge few if any of the new journals have any interest in cognitive science[1].

In 1982 Carbonell and Sleeman established a "techniques and methodology" column in the AI Magazine, whose aim was to help AI mature into a science and maintain its links with cognitive science. By 1987 these subjects are a distinctly minor note in the Magazine, among the product news and exotic applications. The column appears to have been dropped.

The clear trend across the field of fifth generation research is towards formalism, with mathematical, logical and computational analyses of technique taking pride of place over empirical investigations of the ill-defined and difficult issues of cognitve science. In 1987 over 50% of the papers in the journal *artificial intelligence* dealt with this sort of analysis, notably confined to problems of inference and search.

I have no complaint about AI developing as a mature technical discipline. This provides a sound basis for engineering, and some of its results will undoubtedly be practically or conceptually useful to cognitive scientists, but for most in the field the pendulum has swung back from discovery to invention. In short, it seems that many of our colleagues in AI have embraced technology, but simultaneously abandoned science. The computational tradition in cognitive science is weaker in consequence.

Taken together these observations provoke concern. Critics say that Cognitive Psychology leaves gaps in that it fails to address major parts of human experience in perception, understanding, communication and development. At worst it may be irrelevant, misleading and to the extent it is grounded only in experimental paradigms which are subject to fashion it may fail to achieve anything lasting.

The contribution of AI and the computational approach was to provide a complement to experiment; a platform for formulating detailed models of cognition informed by laboratory data, and rigorously testing the sufficiency of theories within complex tasks. The movement of AI and AI scientists towards engineering has reduced the possibility of this happening and left the scientific initiative to be taken by others, presumably psychologists in the main.

Although many psychologists have been intrigued by AI for many years this has not, as we saw earlier, been enough to produce a significant international commitment to symbolic computational modelling. It seems to me that the creation of a strong programme of computationally based theoretical studies, which is informed by empirical studies of human capabilities on nontrivial tasks, and which is designed to complement the already extensive programmes of experimental research, is long overdue and requires vigorous action.

The Case for Computational Modelling

Computer modelling is not just a gloss, a secondary option to doing experiments, occasionally considered as an afterthought, but a productive technique for developing cognitive theory. Three examples of computational work have been selected to support this position.

Cognitive Modelling with Rule Based Systems

Pride of place must be given to the seminal work of Newell and Simon. This started with work on problem solving in the 1950s, reaching a peak with the publication of *Human problem solving* in 1972. At about that time Newell designed a production rule interpreter for use in simulating human problem solving (Newell, 1973b). "PSG" was used extensively for modelling detailed aspects of human information processing on a variety of problems. It influenced many other workers studying a range of complex tasks executed in naturalistic settings. These included imagery (Moran, 1973), children's seviation skills (Young, 1976), mental arithmetic (Young and O'shea, 1981) and decision making (Fox, 1980). Most notably PSG influenced the development of the rule-based ACT model of human information processing (Anderson, 1976; 1983).

The influence of production systems spread beyond theoretical work into applied AI; they influenced work at Stanford University, and the first practical knowledge based expert systems, notably meta-Dendral and MYCIN. PSG also led directly on to the influential OPS series of rule interpreters, used by McDermott and his colleagues to develop R1, a highly successful system designed for a complex task of planning computer installations. The scientific significance of the appearance of practical expert systems is that they have, in turn, motivated a massive growth of interest in, and theoretical understanding of, what is required to solve problems which demand high levels of human knowledge and expertise.

Most significantly these two lines of work, theoretical simulation of cognitive architecture and engineering work on complex, knowledge intensive problem solving, have converged recently in the development of SOAR (Laird, Newell and Rosenbloom, 1987). SOAR embodies the *physical symbol system hypothesis* (Newell, 1981) viz: symbolic systems incorporate all necessary and sufficient means for general intelligence. problem solving is construed as a process of search in a *problem space*, search being controlled by general problem solving methods (e.g. means-ends analysis, hill-climbing) or by specific knowledge appropriate in particular situations.

These ideas are well established. Two additional mechanisms, due to Laird and Rosenbloom, interact to give SOAR a flexibility which is felt to be new to symbolic systems: *universal subgoalinguniversal subgoaling* and *learning by chunking*. The former is a set of mechanisms by which the SOAR software detects an impasse, a point at which it can no longer proceed in its search using specific knowledge. At this point it must generate a problem solving goal through which it can fall back on more general problem solving methods. The learning by chunking mechanism is the complement of universal subgoaling; when SOAR manages to solve a problem it compiles and stores the specific details of the solution it found as a new production rule. Should SOAR find itself in a similar situation this production can be evoked directly, avoiding the impasse and making it unnecessary to solve the problem again.

SOAR is claimed to offer a general architecture for intelligent behaviour which, to date, has been shown to have capabilities ranging from solving small tasks like blocks world tasks and the Wason verification task, to natural language parsing, and knowledge intensive tasks like medical reasoning and configuring computers. Table 1 presents a selection of some of the tasks that SOAR has been applied to. Although it is too early to assess the claim the SOAR group feel that a "unified theory of cognition", which both Neisser and Newell doubted was within the reach of traditional cognitive psychology, can now be seriously contemplated.

Computational Studies of Vision

My second example is in the area of human and computer vision, one of the central topics of psychology and neurophysiology during this century. Visual perception is also a field which has had a destructive propensity for schisms. One of the more notable of these was in visual physiology and psychophysics, between those who regarded the complex and hypercomplex cells found by Hubel and Wiesel as clear demonstrations of a feature-based, "pandemonium" basis of vision, and those seeing the visual system as a set of tuned spatial frequency channels. Perceptual psychology had its divisions too between those who saw the vision research problem in terms of isolating the

TABLE 1
A selection of some of the activities and tasks that the
SOAR architecture has been applied to, taken from Laird,
Newell and Rosenbloom (1987) which should be
consulted for details.

Small, knowledge-lean tasks	Blocks world Tower of Hanoi Missionaries and cannibals problem ...
Small routine tasks	Sequence extrapolation Syllogistic reasoning Wason verification task ...
Knowledge intensive expert system task	Computer configuring Antibacterial therapy advisor ...
Learning (across all tasks SOAR performs)	improvement with practice within/across task transfer strategy acquisition ...

processes of vision - encoding, recognition, attention and so on (Neisser 1967) and those, notably J J Gibson, who saw it in terms of the evolutionary and ecological requirements of vision, and the abilities an organism must have in order to interpret the reflection of light from surfaces, the changing geometry of objects with motion, and so on.

During the sixties and early seventies AI had also addressed the vision problem, producing yet more divisions. For example there were the perceptron and computational geometry of Minsky and Papert at MIT; the description and constraint propagation approaches developed at MIT and Sussex University; the pattern recognition and syntactical approaches at the University of Maryland and so on. By about 1973, however, after a promising start AI vision appeared stuck. The computers at that time had such limited power that scientists were working extensively on cartoon images and polyhedral worlds rather than naturalistic scenes, and being distracted by engineering "tricks", rather than the identification of principles, in their attempts to overcome efficiency problems (perhaps another example of AI's weaknesses in distinguishing science from technology).

The field was unjammed by a scientist who was primarily interested in developing theoretical models of brain function, David Marr. In the early 1970s Marr began to ask a new kind of question, viz, "what is the brain designed to compute? He examined this question in a number of papers on the architecture of human neocortex, hippocampus, and cerebellum. Later, after joining the AI lab at MIT, he took a similar approach to problems of vision. Combining computational concepts from AI with experimental results in visual neurophysiology and perceptual psychology he set a new direction for AI vision (Marr, 1976).

Marr's work profoundly affected visual science. In technology the specialised hardware and image understanding programs which are now set to appear still show the clear contribution of Marr's reformulation of the vision problem. Perhaps his real importance, however, is that he showed how the traditional schisms could all be reconciled. His computational analysis of early visual processing showed how the well known visual cortical units could be viewed as *computing* a fourier transform, while also delivering a symbolic measurement of local features of a natural image. He was simultaneously successful in giving an account of the processes of early vision, and some of the computational constraints on those processes which were imposed by the nature of images.

The Psychology of Decision Making

Many perhaps most decisions involve uncertainty. Traditional thories of decision making have their roots in economics and statistics, and conceive uncertainty within a rationalist framework of mathematical probability. However, it is well known that human decision makers are poor statisticians, and in all likelihood do not make substantial use of quantitative calculations at all in making their decisions. Decision theorists have come to believe that decision makers commonly make use of informal, "heuristic" methods (Kahneman, Slovic and Tversky, 1982) but are inclined to be disdainful about these methods, viewing them as degenerate forms of those prescribed by "rational" or "normative" probability theory.

Observations on the performance of skilled professionals, such as physicians and scientists, suggests that this disdain is somewhat misplaced. In our attempts to design computer systems which offer realistic help to such specialists it is the naivete of "rational" probability theory and decision theories which has become obvious, and in contrast the extraordinary versatility of human reasoning.

The thinking of molecular biologists we work with provides an impressive example. These scientists are trying to predict the three dimensional structure and function of protein molecules. Proteins consist of strings of amino acids which fold up in highly complex and structured ways, to yield an intricate 3-D structure which determines their biological function. This is a complex problem involving great uncertainty but the normal mathematical representations seem much too restrictive. When scientists reason about molecular structure they use an almost bewildering array of devices and methods. Some of the forms of argument and explanatory device they use (and write about) are outlined in table 2. Many heuristics are used to formulate conjectures and predictions about structure and function, and to assess, revise and reject hypotheses using highly coordinated patterns of argument.

These manifold devices generally appear to be used coherently and productively. Uncertainty is explicitly recognised and allowed for, anomalies may cause the very assumptions underlying the problem to be reworked, and so on. Most of these ideas can not be expressed within the language of classical decision theory and mathematical probability; molecular biology is, however, making exciting progress.

We need new ways of thinking about uncertainty and how it is represented and managed in complex problem solving and decision making. Workers in AI are beginning to recognise the need for this and there is considerable growth of interest in symbolic methods for representing uncertainty, including modal logic(e.g. Chellas, 1980), and other non-standard logics (see Smets et al. 1988). There are also good practical arguments for developing a formal semantics for the many "belief terms" which are ubiquitous in human language (Fox, 1985; 1986), and the computational nature of beliefs in terms of inferences and justifications (Cohen, 1985). These developments seem to be corroborating the long and widely held suspicion that there are other rational views of uncertainty than mathematical probability which should be reflected in the psychology of reasoning and decision making (MacDonald, 1986).

New psychological theories of decision making and problem solving are needed which reflect the obvious but critical place of knowledge, and which acknowledge our abilities to reflect on our knowledge, beliefs, justifications and uncertainties. I believe these can only be currently achieved using symbolic computational techniques (Fox, 1984; Fox et al. 1988). They already suggest new kinds of aids for medical problem solving (Fox et al. 1987) and reasoning about molecular structure (Clark and Barton, 1988). It is also possible that this approach may yield a significant clarification of historical arguments about the intuitive foundations of probability itself (Hacking, 1975; Fox, 1986).

TABLE 2

Examples of the wide range of arguments used routinely by molecular biologists reasoning about protein structure.

Structural arguments	e.g. constraints on how objects fill spaces
Causal arguments	e.g. charged amino acids must be on the outside of the molecule
Energetic arguments	e.g. molecular folding tends to minimise free energy

Arguments about the physical influences and constraints which affect the folding process.

Statistical arguments	e.g. inferences from observations of correlated structures
Functional arguments	e.g. function of aggregation is to reduce osmotic pressure
Evolutionary arguments	e.g. structural constraints from conservation of successful substructures
Similarity arguments	e.g. similar functions require similar mechanisms

Arguments which do not model the physical folding process as such, but can be used to constrain search through the space of possible structures.

| *Analogy* | alpha helices are "stiffening rods" protein folding is like dropping a string - produces no knots the lock and key explanation of antibody/antigen and enzyme/substrate interaction structures which are needed to act as "scaffolds" for later folding |

Some arguments which may be merely explanatory devices. They provide models by which to understand molecular folding, though they don't appear to characterise any physical process that influences folding, nor provide any constraints when searching for possible solutions.

Connectionism

In the light of some recent events Neisser's observation about computer modelling that "psychologists simply continue to make theories of other kinds" seems at first sight overstated. In the short period of hullabaloo surrounding the fifth generation another revolution has been emerging; connectionism.

Neural networks, massively parallel computers, distributed computation, connection machines. Here is a set of interrelated ideas which (like everything else) is not new but *is* newly practical. Parallel computation on a large scale has intrigued many people in many disciplines, but achieving it was so impractical that the theories needed to explore and exploit parallelism have not been developed. Like other disciplines psychology has recognised the need for concepts of parallelism for a long time (e.g. Neisser, 1963; Shallice, 1972; Allport, 1977, Barnard, 1986 to name a few) but until recently the development of cognitive theories requiring parallelism could not be developed.

The possibilities offered by new ideas and new parallel computing elements are changing all that. As figure 2 (adapted from figure 1) illustrates many topics previously grouped together under the heading of symbolic computation are now being influenced by parallelism. Ideas of neural nets, perceptrons and so on, which had been more or less abandoned two decades before have now come back into vogue. They were abandoned partly because progress with them had been slow (perhaps because the technology of the time was too limited to explore them properly) but also because of a sophisticated theoretical attack by members of the AI community who were committed to ideas of symbolic computation (notably Minsky and Papert, 1969).

As is well known McClelland, Rumelhart, Hinton and others (McClelland et al. 1986; Rumelhart et al. 1986) have argued that where the computational capabilities of early perceptrons were indeed limited, a slightly more complex form of network incorporating an extra layer of neural units may overcome many of the objections to the early concepts, and offers an intriguing substrate for modelling many cognitive phenomena.

The connectionist outlook is certainly appealing. I have already referred to the need

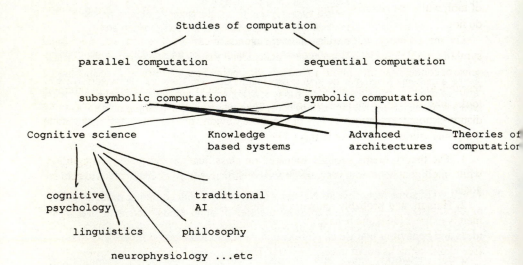

FIG. 7.2   Parallel processing concepts are having a general impact on cognitive science, AI, and computer science. Parallelism is not of itself, however, equivalent to subsymbolic systems.

to explore parallelism for psychological theories. Furthermore the literature seems to be filling up with demonstrations of things that these strangely simple networks can do, from learning genealogies, discovering representational regularities, recognising spoken words and patterns in visual images etc. The fact that they can do these things as well as other current techniques, and they can learn to do these things by simple reinforcement, leads to understandable enthusiasm.

Furthermore if we take the term "neural net" literally it may not be totally naive to think that the connectionist approach could provide a unifying framework for theories of both the mental and physiological mechanisms which underly behaviour (McClelland et al. 1986). Both levels have had equal importance in the history of psychology so the appeal is natural. Traditional AI research (with rare exceptions, such as David Marr's work mentioned above) tends at best to ignore the physical realisation of mental processes, and is often explicitly dualist. Even the "unified theory of cognition" hinted at by the SOAR group seems unlikely to have anything to say about biology.

On the face of it the embrace of connectionism by Cognitive Psychology gives the lie to my concerns about psychology's willingness to develop computational theories. After all you need a computer in order to run these models. Perhaps then I am simply complaining about a decline in the fortunes of my favourite approach, the symbolic approach, since the rise in interest in massively parallel networks is widely interpreted as intrinsically opposed to symbolic theories (e.g. Smolensky, 1986) [2]. Given the right set of ideas, one might say, the experimental community is perfectly willing to make use of tools for computational modelling. It is just that neural nets offer the right sort of tool, while the concepts, languages and research methods of symbolic computation do not.

On the contrary, interesting as connectionist ideas are I assert that traditional symbolic modelling is still necessary, and indeed that it will be impossible to make sense of connectionism without a symbolic viewpoint. I am not criticising connectionist research as such here only observing that to this outsider the connectionist programme looks like one of a number of interesting areas to pursue, while it is receiving disproportionate attention. A few of the more obvious points one might make about the connectionist framework in this context are:

1. The theory seems strongly focussed on classification and pattern recognition, while intelligent behaviour is synthetic and constructive (e.g. we make plans to achieve goals).

2. Human, and probably animal, cognition is reflective. That is to say we do not merely express ideas and behaviour, but we maintain an explicit representation of those ideas and behaviour that we can reflect upon and communicate symbolically to others (see above remarks about uncertainty and decision making in molecular biology).

3. Having a network that does something interesting is not the same as having a theory of why the network does something interesting. As many have complained, neural nets are inscrutable. Until an explicit theory of their principles, competences and limits is available their scientific status is ambiguous.

4. Even if some form of neural net were truly the substrate of cognition, we still have to give epistemological and ontological accounts of the knowledge which informs thinking, problem solving, communication, and so on. AI concepts and techniques of knowledge representation are, at least currently, much better developed for understanding the capabilities underlying intellectual problem solving in such fields as science, medicine etc.[3]

5. The learning abilities of these networks are their most compelling feature, however there are also interesting learning theories developed within the physical symbol system framework. The obvious example is SOAR's mechanism of learning by chunking.

I conclude that, whatever the historical significance of neural networks will prove to be, they are unlikely to displace the physical symbol system hypothesis; some sort of cohabitation of symbolic and subsymbolic concepts seems desirable.

CONCLUSIONS

To recapitulate, I have argued that the transmogrification of AI from science to engineering, and the rise in connectionism are causing an undesirable reduction in cognitive modelling of the symbolic kind. I have recalled some old, but still forceful, arguments that motivated the original rise of computational modelling, and mustered a few recent ones to suggest that connectionism is not really a substitute. This is a time when the physical symbol system hypothesis is making real progress; cognitive science needs thoughtful management to maintain and encourage its development.

NOTES

1 One exception being *The knowledge engineering Review* which is edited by the author.
2 Though it is not at all clear that the founders of the movement feel the same way.
3 Though admittedly problem solving which is informed by "common sense" is proving much more intractable. Conceivably subsymbolic mechanisms have a particular contribution here.

ACKNOWLEDGEMENTS

I would like to thank Alan Baddeley, Tim Shallice, and particularly the anonymous referees for comments which helped me to greatly improve this commentary.

REFERENCES

Allport, A. (1977). On knowing the meaning of words we are unable to report: The effects of visual masking. *Attention and Performance IV*, 505-545.
Anderson, J. R. (1976). *Language, Memory and Thought*. Hillsdale, New Jersey: Erlbaum Associates
Anderson, J. R. (1983). *The architecture of cognition*. Cambridge, Massachusetts: Harvard.
Barnard, P. J. (1986). Interacting cognitive subsystems: A psycholinguistic approach to short term memory. In Ellis, A (ed.) *Progress in the psychology of language vol 2*, 197–258. London: Lawrence Erlbaum.
Carbonell, J. & Sleeman, D. (1982). AI Techniques and Methodology. *The AI Magazine*, Spring, p47.
Chellas, B. F. (1986). Modal logic: An introduction. Cambridge: Cambridge University and Press. 1980

Clark, D. & Barton, G. (1988). Knowledge engineering in the CARDS project: a report on work in progress. ICRF Biomedical Computing Unit Technical report.

Cohen, P. (1985). *Heuristic reasoning about uncertainty: An Artificial Intelligence Approach*. London: Pitman.

Fox, J. (1980). Making decisions under the influence of memory. *Psychological Review, 87(2)*, 190-211.

Fox, J. (1984). Formal and knowledge-based Methods in decision technology. *Acta Psychologica, 56*, 303-331.

Fox, J. (1985). Three arguments for extending the framework of probability. In L. N. Kanal & J. F. Lemmer (Eds) *Uncertainty in Artificial Intelligence*. Amsterdam: North Holland.

Fox, J. (1986). Making decisions under the influence of knowledge. In P. Morris (Ed). *Modelling Cognition*. London: Wiley.

Fox, J., Glowinski, A., O'Neil, M. (1987). A prototype knowledge based information system for primary care. In J. Fox, M. Fieschi and R. Engelbrecht (Eds). *Proceedings of European Conference on AI in medicine*. Marseilles, Berlin: Springer-Verlag.

Fox, J., O'Neil, M., Glowinski, A. J., & Clark, D. (1988, to appear). A logic of decision making. International Interdisciplinary Workshop on Decision Making. University of Illinois, Urbana-Champaign.

Hacking, I. (1975). *The emergence of probability*. Cambridge: Cambridge University Press.

Kahneman, D., Slovic, P. & Tversky, A. (1982). *Judgement under uncertainty: Heuristics and biases*. Cambridge: Cambridge University Press.

Laird, J. E., Newell, A. & Rosenbloom, P. S. (1987). SOAR: An architecture for general intelligence. *Artificial Intelligence, 33*, pp 1-64.

Macdonald, R. (1986). Credible conceptions and implausible probabilities. *British Journal of Mathematical and Statistical Psychology, 39*, 15-27.

Marr, D. (1976). Early processing of visual information. *Phil. Trans. Roy. Soc. Lond. B, 275*, 483-524.

McClelland, J. L. & Rumelhart, D. E. (Eds) (1986). *Parallel Distributed Processing Vol 2*. Cambridge: MIT Press.

Minsky, M. & Papert, S. (1969). *Perceptions*, Cambridge: MIT Press

Moran, T. P. (1973). The symbolic imagery hypothesis Unpublished dissertation, Carnegie-Mellon University, Pittsburg, PA.

Neisser, U. (1963). The multiplicity of thought. *British Journal of Psychology, 54*, 1-14.

Neisser, U. (1967). *Cognitive Psychology*. New York: Appleton Century Crofts.

Neisser, U. (1976). *Cognition and Reality*. San Francisco: Freeman.

Newell, A. (1973a). You can't play twenty questions with nature and win. In W. Chase (ed.). *Visual information Processing*. New York: Academic Press.

Newell, A. (1973b). Production systems: Models of control structures. In W. Chase (ed.). *Visual Information Processing* New York: Academic Press.

Newell, A. & Simon, H. A. (1972). *Human Problem Solving*. Englewood Cliffs, New Jersey: Prentice-Hall.

Newell, A. (1981). The Knowledge Level. *The AI Magazine, Summer 1981* pp 1-20.

Norman, D. A. (1981). What is cognitive science? In D. A. Normal (Ed.) *Perspectives on Cognitive Science*. Norwood, New Jersey: Ablex.

Rawlings Rumelhart, D. E. & McClelland, J. L. (Eds.) (1986). *Parallel Distributed Processing vol 2*. Cambridge: MIT Press..

Shallice, T. (1972). Dual functions of consciousness. *Psychological Review, 79(5)*, 383-393.

Smets, P., Mamdani, E. H., Dubois, D., Prade, H. (1988). *Non-standard logics for automated reasoning*. London: Academic Press.

Smolensky, P. (1986). Information processing in dynamical systems: Foundations of harmony theory. In Rumelhart, McClelland, et al. (Eds.) *Parallel Distributed Processing*. Cambridge: MIT Press.

Young, R. M. (1976). *Seriation by children: An AI analysis of a Piagetian task*. Basle: Birkhauser.

Young, R. M., & O'shea, T. (1981). Errors in children's subtraction. *Cognitive Science vol 5*, pp 153-177.

Author Index

Subject Index